LEGAL, REGULATORY
AND GOVERNANCE ISSUES
IN ISLAMIC FINANCE

Edinburgh Guides to Islamic Finance
Series Editor: Rodney Wilson

A series of short guides to key areas in Islamic finance, offering an independent academic perspective and a critical treatment.

Product Development in Islamic Banks
Habib Ahmed

Shariʻah Compliant Private Equity and Islamic Venture Capital
Fara Madeha Ahmad Farid

Shariʻah *Governance in Islamic Banks*
Zulkifli Hasan

Islamic Financial Services in the United Kingdom
Elaine Housby

Islamic Asset Management
Natalie Schoon

Legal, Regulatory and Governance Issues in Islamic Finance
Rodney Wilson

Forthcoming
Islamic and Ethical Finance in the United Kingdom
Elaine Housby

www.euppublishing.com/series/egif

LEGAL, REGULATORY AND GOVERNANCE ISSUES IN ISLAMIC FINANCE

Rodney Wilson

EDINBURGH
University Press

Edinburgh University Press Ltd
22 George Square, Edinburgh EH8 9LF
www.euppublishing.com

Typeset in Minion Pro by
Servis Filmsetting Ltd, Stockport, Cheshire, and
printed and bound in Great Britain by
CPI Group (UK) Ltd, Croydon CR0 4YY

A CIP record for this book is available from the British Library

ISBN 978 0 7486 4505 3 (hardback)
ISBN 978 0 7486 4504 6 (paperback)
ISBN 978 0 7486 4506 0 (webready PDF)
ISBN 978 0 7486 5527 4 (epub)
ISBN 978 0 7486 5526 7 (Amazon ebook)

CONTENTS

Tables

Figures

CHAPTER 1
INTRODUCTION

The governance of Islamic finance is at the intersection of national and *Shari'ah* law, resulting in a wide variety of interpretations in different jurisdictions. These differences have implications for the regulatory systems under which Islamic financial institutions operate, with considerable variations in practices between countries. This complexity can result in uncertainty and even confusion, and there have been calls for the standardisation of Islamic financial contracts. However the variations in regulation and in the contracts offered has resulted in healthy debate about the merits of different approaches, and it is this which has driven the Islamic finance industry forward during the last four decades.

The aim of this guide is to explain how the complexities have arisen and why there is no single governance system which is suitable for all types of Islamic financial institutions or for the contracts which they offer. Although *Shari'ah* law on issues such as inheritance is detailed and precise, for most types of legal contracts it is concerned with general principles. Financial contracts are judged in terms of how equitable is the treatment of the different parties, and the extent to which the outcomes are fair and just. Islamic financial contracts have a moral purpose, and are not simply concerned with maximising the pecuniary benefits of the signatories.

Islamic financial contracts are usually drafted by qualified lawyers either working for a law firm or within an Islamic financial institution. The legal work involved is the same as that when a conventional financial contract is drafted, the stress being on issues such as providing appropriate provision for what happens in cases of payments default, or how disagreements between the parties can be handled. What makes Islamic financial contracts different is that they are subject to scrutiny by a board of *fiqh* scholars conversant with Muslim jurisprudence to ensure that they are *Shari'ah* compliant. This involves the scholars satisfying themselves that the contracts are free from *riba* in all its forms, which can be interpreted as an addition to a sum lent, usually equated with interest. The scholars will be also concerned that there is no *gharar* or legal uncertainty in the contract, which would be present if there were clauses capable of ambiguous interpretation that could be exploited by one of the parties at the expense of the others.

Islamic contractual principles

It is important to note that Islamic jurisprudence is not only concerned with the enforcement of *Shari'ah* prohibitions in the wording of contracts, such as those on *riba* and *gharar*, but also with how financing is structured and how it is used. Financing is seen as a tool and not an end in itself, the concern being that merely making money from money is inherently unjust as it serves no useful purpose. Rather, financing should be used to facilitate productive activity that enhances the output of socially desirable goods and services and contributes to the creation of meaningful and respectable employment opportunities.

Returns from financing and investment have to be justified under *Shari'ah* law, and this can either be through work and effort or risk sharing.[1] There are costs involved in appraising the viability of projects for which funding is requested and in estimating the risks involved. There are also administrative costs in arranging the disbursement of funds and the collection of repayments and service charges. Legal costs include those involved in drafting contracts and getting them approved by qualified scholars of *fiqh*. It is recognised that Islamic financial institutions have to cover these overheads and at the same time generate profits for their depositors and shareholders. Therefore Islamic financing is not necessarily cheaper than its conventional equivalent, and in some cases can actually prove more costly because of the additional provision for *Shari'ah* compliance. However, as a matter of good practice there should be transparency over how the costs are calculated and contractual certainty about what liabilities the client obtaining funding is actually taking on.

An important principle of Islamic finance is that commercial risks, which are seen as inevitable, should be shared rather than transferred to a weaker party who could be potentially exploited.[2] The assumption is that burdens should be shared by the contracting parties, or in other words there should be brotherly solidarity which can itself be a source of strength. To achieve this it is not merely a matter of modifying conventional contracts, such as those governing loans, which if undertaken for purely commercial motives will never result in an equitable outcome. Rather, it may involve structuring new contracts, drawing upon the principles of traditional *fiqh*, but worded to comply with national laws and enforceable through state courts. Such contracts are described as being *Shari'ah* based, and include *murabaha* purchase and sales contracts, *ijara* operating leases, *istisna* project financing, *wakala* agency agreements and *mudaraba* and *musharaka* partnership contracts, all of which are discussed in Chapters 3 and 4. The characteristics these contracts have in common are that they involve a degree of risk and profit sharing and facilitate real economic activity.

Conventional financial contracts can be accepted under *Shari'ah* law even where they are not based on traditional *fiqh* principles. Hence, equity investment contracts are usually acceptable, even though the motivation of the investors is often to make capital gains rather than simply receive a share of any profit. The *Shari'ah*-compliant funds discussed in Chapter 8 largely invest in equities, including private equity as well as shares in listed companies. Note that such contracts are deemed to be *Shari'ah* compliant, not *Shari'ah* based. However, to be *Shari'ah* compliant the investment must be in companies engaged in *halal* or permitted activities rather than those engaged in *haram* or forbidden pursuits, such as lending with interest or the production and distribution of alcohol deemed intoxicating or pork products regarded as unclean.

If the *fiqh* scholars are satisfied that contracts are indeed *Shari'ah* compliant, or even better *Shari'ah* based, they issue a *fatwa* or ruling to indicate to the parties that the contract complies with Islamic law. This signals that the agreements can be signed by the parties with a clear conscience. It is the *fiqh* scholars who will ultimately be accountable to the Almighty for what they have approved, not the contracting parties who have accepted the *fatwa* as a matter of trust. This of course raises issues concerning the moral legitimacy of the *Shari'ah* vetting and approval processes, matters that will be considered in greater detail in Chapter 2.

Legal challenges for Islamic financial institutions

Most Islamic financial institutions operate under existing bank laws and regulations without any special provision. The exceptions include Iran, where all banking is subject to the Law on Usury-Free Banking, which is discussed in detail in Chapter 5, and Malaysia and Indonesia, where there are special laws governing Islamic banking, and in the case of Malaysia, also a law governing Islamic *takaful* insurance. These laws are discussed in Chapter 6, where the provision in Kuwait is also considered, as it involved a significant addition to the existing banking law. In these jurisdictions Islamic banks compete with conventional banks operating under laws that provide for interest-based lending, such situations normally being described as dual systems.

Legal disputes over Islamic financial contracts will normally be dealt with by national courts and not *Shari'ah* courts whose remit is confined to family matters such as divorce or inheritance. As most disputes involve non-payment of financial obligations and breaches of contract, it can be argued that there is no justification for treating Islamic bank clients differently to those of conventional banks. However, there are differences as Islamic banking is subject to religious injunctions whereas conventional contracts are not. Of particular relevance to cases of default is the following quotation from the Quran:

> If the debtor is in difficulty, grant him time till it is easy for him to repay. If ye remit by way of charity that is best for you if ye only knew. (*Sura* 2: 280)

Such provisions are unlikely to be explicitly written into Islamic financial contracts, but as the Quran is the ultimate source of Islamic law, and as the contracts are designated as *Shari'ah* compliant, the religious teaching cannot be ignored.

The signatories to the contracts who have obtained financing could potentially cite this injunction if they fail to make the necessary repayments, arguing that if they are given time, they will meet their obligations. How should the court and the Islamic bank itself respond? If the judge takes the position that because the bank is Islamic, it should exercise leniency, this could result in the Islamic bank being placed at a competitive disadvantage to its conventional counterparts seeking full and prompt repayments. The court could be enforcing payments by the defaulter in the latter case, perhaps even by the handover of collateral or the sale of assets, while the defaulter of the Islamic bank is not subject to such measures, and perhaps escapes justice.

Where clients have financing from both Islamic and conventional banks there is the danger that they might give priority to repaying their interest-based loans first rather than honouring their Islamic financing obligations. This moral hazard problem has long been a challenge for Islamic banks, which unscrupulous clients may regard as a soft touch.[3] When clients are late in making payments on loans, conventional banks charge additional interest, and such late payment obligations are usually specified in the credit agreements. Islamic financial institutions cannot impose such late payment penalties as the additions would constitute *riba*. Charging interest on the capital owed is itself condemned, and charging interest on unpaid interest soon results in a debt spiral which becomes exploitative.

The terms and conditions for Islamic financing have to be specified in the contract which the parties freely sign. In the case of major financing deals there will be negotiation between the parties rather than the standard contracts used for retail and small-business finance. In either case, once the contract is agreed and signed, the parties are bound by its terms. Repayment delays or defaults constitute a breach of contract unless provision is specifically made for such contingencies. This can involve specifying the circumstances under which a standstill agreement can come into force in the original contract rather than trying to negotiate such an agreement after a payments default. Of course the implicit recognition of credit risk would therefore be built into the contract, which would be priced accordingly. In other words, the funding may cost more than conventional financing, but the client may believe it is worth paying a premium to reduce financing risk and avoid *gharar*, which is often present in conventional contracts, and which becomes all too apparent when relations between the parties break down as a result of contractual disputes.

Those who receive Islamic finance of course take on some risk; indeed, given that risk sharing is an essential Islamic principle it is desirable that clients assume this burden.[4] As an important attribute for successful business is skilled risk management, it is both equitable and efficient that risk should be shared. Islamic financial contracts that simply mimic the terms of their conventional equivalents are more likely to result in defaults, especially if the costs are based on interest. As interest rates are determined at the macro-economic level, usually as a result of decisions on monetary policy, business managers will have no comparative advantage in assessing such risk. In contrast, business risks at the micro level will affect the amount of profit to be shared with the financier, and in this business managers should be well placed to influence profitability and predict future performance.

Of course there will always be unanticipated contingencies that could cause defaults, even with Islamic financial contracts. Where these are the result of poor business judgements and the clients breach their contracts, there is no reason why they should not be held liable for their repayments obligations. Where the default results from fraudulent practices or deception then the client should be liable not only for the contractual obligations for the financing, but arguably for compensation to the Islamic bank through fines or other penalties, including all legal costs. In extreme circumstances criminal prosecutions may also be justified, especially if the fraudulent behaviour has damaged the public interest, including those of Islamic bank depositors. In such cases imprisonment may be the outcome both to punish the defendant and as a deterrent to others.

If, however, the client is unable to meet their obligations because of unexpected illness or family crises, then there is a case for leniency, and for giving the debtor time to repay as stipulated in *Sura* 2: 280. In extreme cases of misfortune there may also be an argument for remission 'by way of charity', or in other words debt forgiveness. This of course will imply that the Islamic bank has to make complete provision for the bad debt, which may result in losses, clearly a practice that cannot be undertaken lightly or repeated too often. Ultimately the Islamic bankers will have to make a moral judgement, conditioned by *fiqh*, that the case for granting debt forgiveness outweighs their responsibilities to depositors and shareholders.

Is a different regulatory system required?

The three aims of bank regulation are firstly to protect the interests of depositors, secondly to encourage fare competition to keep down financing costs and thirdly to ensure that banks do not fail and require support from government using taxpayers money. These objectives are the same for Islamic banks as for their conventional counterparts, reinforcing the case for them being regulated in the same manner. Furthermore, the risks faced by conventional banks, such as credit, liquidity and operational risk, also apply to Islamic banks. Risk management issues facing the regulatory authorities will be considered in greater detail in Chapter 7.

Islamic banks are confronted with additional risks to those experienced in conventional banking, notably the reputational risks associated with *Shari'ah* compliance; ownership risks arising from certain types of financial contracts, namely those covering *murabaha* and *ijara*; and market risk depending on how *musharaka* is structured and the exit conditions. For regulatory authorities the challenge is how such risks can be best managed, and whether there are any skill and organisational issues for the central banks themselves. As in all jurisdictions there can only be one regulatory authority for banks this implies that there can be no separate regulatory authority for Islamic banks. Therefore, the usual approach is to establish a division or department within the regulatory authority either to advise on the issues pertaining to Islamic banks or to actually undertake the regulation.

In some jurisdictions such as Malaysia, Pakistan and the Sudan the central banks have established their own *Shari'ah* boards which can advise, or in some circumstances, enforce controls over *Shari'ah* compliance policies and procedures within the regulated institutions. Arguably this can serve to mitigate *Shari'ah* compliance risk and enhance reputational confidence by having a national policy rather than the reputational risk being associated with an individual Islamic financial institution at the micro level. The central bank's *Shari'ah* board can vet appointments to *Shari'ah* boards of the regulated banks, ensuring those appointed are appropriately qualified and experienced. They can also provide definitive rulings when there are irreconcilable differences between members of the *Shari'ah* board of a regulated institution. In addition they can promote consistency in *Shari'ah* board rulings.

Most jurisdictions do not, however, have national *Shari'ah* boards, the counterargument being that they impose a straight jacket on *fatwa*, add to bureaucracy and discourage debate and innovation. There are often conflicting *fatwa* by the *Shari'ah* boards of different Islamic financial institutions, even within the same jurisdiction, and *Shari'ah* boards often change their opinions, resulting in inconsistency over time and uncertainty over precedent. Nevertheless, many feel these are prices worth paying to have institutional autonomy and the flexibility to offer different types of contracts to serve the needs of the clients of particular Islamic financial institutions.

Regulatory authorities worldwide are used to dealing with the credit risk which arises in conventional lending. There are international standards through Basel II and III as to how non-performing loans should be treated which will be considered in detail in Chapter 7. These rules also apply to financing by Islamic banks, even though they are not involved in interest-based lending.[5] Although this has not proved a problem, the identical treatment from a regulatory perspective of non-performing debt, whether conventional or Islamic, is a factor explaining why all too often Islamic financial contracts mimic their conventional equivalents. In other words, the lack of regulatory challenges, although welcome, is a result of Islamic banks trying to make their financial products compatible with the existing systems rather than the regulatory authorities adapting and devising systems that would better accommodate the Islamic financial principle of risk sharing.

In particular, bank regulators are often unhappy about,

and are uncertain how to manage, the ownership and market risks that inevitably arise in Islamic finance if the products are to be *Shari'ah* based. Specifically, ownership risk is an inherent and essential component of *murabaha* and *ijara* contracts which account for a major share of Islamic banking activity. In practice Islamic banks seek to mitigate ownership risks, either by ownership passing to the client immediately after a *murabaha* contract comes into force, or by the *ijara* contract being given many of the characteristics of a financing rather than an operating lease. There is a view amongst some regulators that *ijara* would be better undertaken by leasing companies rather than banks given the ownership risks involved. Leasing companies are subject to much less scrutiny as their funding comes from their shareholders and not from depositors as is the case with banks.

Market risk arises in *mudaraba* and *musharaka* contracts if these are structured according to Islamic financial principles as the exit value for the financier cannot be guaranteed as is the case with debt finance, whether Islamic or conventional. However, in practice many regulators prefer to see exit values predetermined rather than dependent on market developments, or in other words *mudaraba* and *musharaka* becoming more debt- rather than equity-type contracts. Islamic banks can, and indeed do, argue that as a high proportion of their liabilities are in investment *mudaraba* deposits, the value of which cannot be guaranteed, rather than current accounts, which represent predetermined and fixed liabilities, they have more flexibility than conventional banks, all of whose deposit obligations are predetermined when the deposits are made. Hence if investment *mudaraba* deposit liabilities are matched in whole or in part by *mudaraba* and *musharaka* assets, market risk should not be a problem.

In reality it is unlikely that the market-risk profile of the liabilities and assets will match, not least because investment *mudaraba* depositors will never want to see the value of their deposits written down. Given this reality from a regulatory perspective such deposits are treated as identical to conventional savings accounts. Therefore, if the value of liabilities is treated as a fixed obligation, this will have implications for the corresponding assets, hence the demand that they become debt instruments rather than equity. These issues will be considered further in Chapter 3 where the terms and conditions governing Islamic bank deposits will be explored in greater detail.

Implications of participatory finance for stakeholders and governance

This guide also covers governance issues including the responsibilities of the *Shari'ah* boards in the governance structures and the status of investment *mudaraba* depositors compared with shareholders, as it is the latter who are the owners of the Islamic bank. Clearly, in principle, there are significant differences between the types of governance structure appropriate for Islamic financial institutions in comparison to conventional institutions. There are also implications for the responsibilities and status of the different stakeholder groups with consequences for inputs into institutional decision making and the overall power structure.

The difference between theory and practice are as apparent for Islamic financial governance at the institutional level as they are at the regulatory level. The consequences of participatory finance, an essential feature of any Islamic financial system, for corporate governance have yet to be fully explored. In Chapter 11 the discussion is taken further, but here it is appropriate to highlight some of the issues.

Participatory finance concerns risk and reward sharing, the issues being how this is accomplished and who gets what. There are inevitably conflicts of interest between different stakeholders in an Islamic financial institution just as there are in a conventional bank, but in the case of the former some of the conflicts are different and require particular types of management. As it is the corporate governance structure that provides the framework for the management of potential conflicts of interest, this will be distinctive in the case of Islamic financial institutions. The potential conflict over profit shares between investment *mudaraba* depositors and shareholders, for example, does not arise in conventional banks. There the issue is how much interest to pay to savings-account holders but this is directly influenced by the cost of central bank funding which is largely determined by their monetary policy stance. Hence interest rates can be regarded as an exogenous variable related to macroeconomic policy.

In contrast, the profit proportion paid to investment *mudaraba* depositors will depend on what is deemed to be a fair division of profits between them and the shareholders. This proportion is determined endogenously within the Islamic financial institution itself, subject of course to paying a competitive return to depositors while maintaining a dividend to shareholders which is sufficient to ensure that they continue to hold their investment rather than selling the shares. In other words, the profit-sharing proportions between the Islamic bank and its depositors are determined at the microeconomic level. It will be for the Board of Directors to reconcile shareholder and depositor interests, in contrast to the position of a conventional bank where the Board only represents the former. The implications for corporate governance may be that the Board of Directors needs to be differently constituted for Islamic banks as there is not only the classic agency conflict between management insiders and external shareholders, but also a third party, the investment *mudaraba* depositors, who are also direct participants in the bank and whose income will be directly dependent on the profit shares agreed. Arguably their participation would be more meaningful if they have their own representatives on the Board of Directors, a governance innovation that most Islamic banks have yet to take on board.

It can be argued that if the *Shariʿah* board is allowed to nominate at least one member, possibly its chairman, to serve on the Board of Directors, this could be a way of serving the interests of the investment *mudaraba* depositors. There is an argument in any case, irrespective of serving particular stakeholder groups, for having such representation on the Board of Directors; firstly, that the *Shariʿah* scholars could give advice on matters of *fiqh* where an immediate opinion is required, rather than waiting for the *Shariʿah* board to meet. Second, there is the argument that the *Shariʿah* member of the Board of Directors would have oversight of what decisions were being made at the top of the organisation and could participate in the deliberations over those decisions. A counterargument is that the skills of the *Shariʿah* scholars are in *fiqh*, not in strategic management, the main function of the Board of Directors. Nor are the scholars' skills in financial matters which might be relevant to the profit share allocated to investment *mudaraba* depositors.

These issues will be further discussed in Chapters 3 and 11. In the next chapter the focus is on national laws and the legal framework under which Islamic financial institutions function and how it accommodates *Shariʿah* in both principle and practice.

Notes

1. Rodney Wilson, 'Islam', in Jan Peil and Irene van Staveren (eds), *Handbook of Economics and Ethics* (Cheltenham: Edward Elgar, 2009), pp. 283–90.

2. Rodney Wilson, 'Economy', in Amyn B. Sajoo (ed.), *A Companion to Muslim Ethics* (London: I. B. Tauris, 2010), pp. 131–50.

3. Abdel-Hameed Bashir, 'Limited liability, moral hazard and financial constraints in profit sharing contracts', in Munawar Iqbal (ed.), *Islamic Banking and Finance: Current Developments in Theory and Practice* (Leicester: Islamic Foundation, 2001), pp. 105–25.

4. Muhammad Nejatullah Siddiqi, *Partnership and Profit Sharing in Islamic Law* (Leicester: Islamic Foundation, 1985), pp. 19–37.

5. Mansoor Shakil, 'The impact of Basel II on Islamic banking', in S. Nazim Ali (ed.), *Islamic Finance: Current Legal and Regulatory Issues* (Cambridge, MA: Harvard Law School, 2005), pp. 153–66.

CHAPTER 2
COMMON LAW, CIVIL LAW AND *SHARI'AH*

Islamic financial contracts are subject to two different types of scrutiny before they can be approved, as on the one hand they must be compatible with *Shari'ah*, and on the other they must comply with national legal and regulatory requirements and be enforceable in the courts. This double scrutiny involves both *Shari'ah* scholars trained in *fiqh muamalat*, that branch of Islamic law concerned with worldly transactions and everyday living, and qualified lawyers trained in commercial law. There are obviously few problems in drafting and enforcing contracts where *Shari'ah* and national laws are compatible, but major challenges, if not impossible obstacles, if the two types of law conflict.

Where there are conflicts if contracts are to be offered either the *Shari'ah* scholars will have to alter their positions, or national laws and regulations will have to be amended or revised. Some critics of the Islamic financial contracts currently offered believe that the *Shari'ah* scholars have compromised their position too much. Others assert that unless there is a political willingness to change national laws and regulations to accommodate Islamic finance, such services should not be offered. An extreme position is to argue that the Islamic financial contracts lack *Shari'ah* creditability, and therefore they should not be offered. This is a rather defeatist approach that would result in there being no alternative to interest-based finance and which would make the entire Islamic finance industry redundant.

As this guide will illustrate, despite legal and regulatory obstacles in many jurisdictions, contracts are offered based on Islamic financial principles, which although not ideal in practice from a *Shari'ah* perspective, are nevertheless a real alternative to contracts based on *riba*. *Shari'ah* scrutiny can also minimise if not eliminate *gharar*, work welcomed by the regulatory authorities in all jurisdictions. The major potential areas of conflict with legal requirements and regulation arise with respect to deposit protection, an issue covered in Chapter 3, and the ownership and market risks arising in some types of Islamic financing contracts, matters covered in Chapter 4 where the terms of such contracts are examined and Chapter 7 which focuses on Islamic bank regulation.

National laws and the universal *Shari'ah*

All Islamic financial institutions are established under national laws and the contracts they issue are governed by these laws. Normally the laws only apply in the jurisdictions in which they are enacted, as extending the remit of the laws to other jurisdictions would be regarded as an interference with national sovereignty by other governments. There are no international laws pertaining to Islamic finance or indeed any other type of finance, although there are regulatory standards, notably those developed through the Bank for International Settlements and set out in the Basel I, II and III agreements, which most national regulatory bodies adhere to in order to ensure that the institutions they regulate are viewed by foreign financial institutions as creditworthy counterparties. These regulations apply to both Islamic and conventional banks but for the former the Kuala Lumpur-based Islamic Financial Services Board (IFSB) has produced useful guidelines as to how international agreements such as Basel II can be applied.

In contrast to national laws which are jurisdiction specific, *Shari'ah* law is God given and universal. Muslims, irrespective of wherever they work or reside, are obliged to adhere to *Shari'ah* law.[1] Hence they have a dual obligation to respect both the national laws of the countries of which they are citizens and the moral law of Islam which governs the lives of the faithful, including their financial dealings. National laws govern the operation of Islamic financial institutions and Islamic financial contracts in both Muslim-majority and Muslim-minority countries. There are, however, no institutions at international level, or even national level, to enact laws based on the principles of *Shari'ah*.

Although in some Muslim-majority countries the religion of Islam is referred to in the constitutions, usually the implication is that all laws should be consistent with Islamic teaching, which is very different to decreeing that all laws should be Islamic. In other words, laws are enacted if these are regarded as being in the national interest, and as part of this process there may (or may not) be an opportunity for Muslim scholars to give their views. This contrasts with the approach of enacting specific laws to enforce Islamic moral teaching in areas such as financial transactions, an approach that is rarely taken.

As shall be shown in Chapter 5 Iran has a specific Islamic banking law, and all laws passed, including the Usury-Free Banking Law of 1983, were subject to scrutiny by the Council of Moral Guardians, which functions rather like an upper house of parliament or senate, although it is appointed rather than elected. In contrast, in Saudi Arabia, although the country is the heartland of Islam and its ruler is designated as custodian of the two holy shrines, there is no legal provision for Islamic banking and there was no religious scrutiny of the Banking Control Law of 1996.

National laws are socially determined rather than God given, as they may be enacted to ensure there is a degree of social justice to encourage the majority to respect and obey the law. As over time what is socially acceptable changes, national laws are inevitably amended or even replaced, often as a result of political pressures. In contrast *Shari'ah* principles are eternal, as Divine teaching does not change. However, as new circumstances arise Islamic scholars have to investigate how best to apply the principles of *Shari'ah*, and it is this application that changes, not the Divine law itself.

Secular laws often reflect political compromises and set minimum standards, but are far from being idealistic. Yet the Islamic finance movement has always been idealistic and deeply concerned with morality. The central concern is with what is *halal*, literally righteous, and what is *haram*, or impermissible. *Shari'ah* law reconciles private and public interest and for the faithful its implementation is believed to bring social harmony. Islamic teaching stresses religious obligations rather than private rights, which may ultimately be associated with selfishness and greed, especially in the financial sphere. In contrast, although secular laws may reflect and attempt to express the social aspirations of the citizens of a country, in practice their behaviour reflects their own private interests and those of their families rather than those of the wider community.

Shari'ah is usually referred to as law, but it is very different to national legal precepts in terms of its aims and practices. Indeed in some respects it may be a more accurate English interpretation to refer to *Shari'ah* principles or *Shari'ah* teaching rather than *Shari'ah* law. In particular, respect for *Shari'ah* is concerned with determining the right way or ways for financial dealings where right is interpreted in a moral sense and distinguished from wrong or sinful. Citizens can abide by national laws, yet behave in an immoral way, including in financial dealings where laws are unable to curb speculative behaviour or the exploitation of the gullible.

As *Shari'ah* is a moral code the stress for the faithful is on obedience through submission to the Will of the Almighty, whereas with national law the emphasis is on observance, even where the citizen disagrees with what the law states. Observance is a matter of legal necessity, but not an act of faith. It is conscience that ensures compliance with *Shari'ah*, but compliance with national laws is because of the threat of punishment involving fines, imprisonment or worse. Compliance is necessary whether the national law is just or unjust, an issue that never arises with *Shari'ah* which is inherently just. As a consequence there is willing compliance by Muslims with *Shari'ah* whereas compliance with national laws may be half hearted or even minimalist, involving form rather than substance.

Customary law and common law

Long before the arrival of Islam laws existed, as if society is to function and anarchy cease to prevail, some sort of legal code has to prevail. In the Arabian Peninsula, as elsewhere, it was tribal law that was the norm, as the tribe was the social unit. Tribal law is often referred to as customary law, as it has evolved over the many centuries that mankind has inhabited the earth, often with disputes between tribal members being resolved to the satisfaction of the tribe, and setting a precedent for other later dispute resolution. It was the tribal elders who adjudicated: those with the greatest experience of dispute resolution who enjoyed the confidence of the entire tribe. They played a leadership role, but did not exercise judicial power in an arbitrary manner, but rather with reference to previous tribal norms and customs.

Customary law is regarded as having a wider remit than tribal law. The latter may be applied for intratribal disputes, but where disputes are intertribal and there are conflicting tribal practices, there is the question of what tribal precedent should apply. Obviously tribal power may be significant, with the precedents of the dominant tribe applying, but whether these ensure just outcomes may be debatable. It may in any case be more fruitful to look at the precedents set by a number of tribal groups and at previous intertribal disputes, assuming there are records of these and that the knowledge is disseminated. Once this happens and there is general tribal consent, this will form the basis for customary law which may eventually be applied at national level once the tribal groupings evolve into or are subordinated to more centralised states.

Common law has its roots in custom and precedent and can be regarded as a further evolution of customary law. It evolved in England during the Middle Ages and is therefore frequently referred to as English Common Law. Countries that were part of the British Empire and trace their legal inheritance to England use English Common Law. Their jurisdictions include many countries with Muslim-majority populations such as Pakistan, Bangladesh and Malaysia, and countries with substantial Muslim populations such as Nigeria. In all these jurisdictions English Common Law has absorbed and complemented local customary laws, a fusion that forms the basis of their national legal systems. How these relate to *Shari'ah* is a central concern of this study.

English Common Law is also widely used internationally for financial contracts, not least because of the significance of London as an international financial centre, and New York and Singapore as financial centres. Both the United States and Singapore were former colonies of the United Kingdom and therefore have legal systems based on English Common Law. As a result of the dominance globally of English Common Law governance for financial contracts and transactions aspiring financial centres usually adopt this as their law of choice. Hence, in the Gulf, both the Dubai International Financial Centre and the Qatar Financial Centre have adopted English Common Law. This applies even though the United Arab Emirates and Qatar, like other Arab countries, have legal practices based on civil law, which will be discussed later.

Another factor favouring the adoption of English Common Law for financial contracts is that the leading international commercial law firms are based in London and New York, but have gradually established global networks that include offices throughout the Muslim world and in major centres for Islamic finance such as Bahrain, Dubai and Kuala Lumpur. It is these firms that draft most Islamic finance contracts, from deposit contracts based on *mudaraba* for retail savers to the *sukuk* contracts arranged by investment banks for sovereign states and large business corporations. All these contracts are drafted to be enforceable in English Common Law jurisdictions as well as being compatible with *Shari'ah*.

Common law exists alongside and compliments statutory law and it would be misleading to view the two as being in conflict. Rather it is statutory law which provides the legal framework which the judiciary interpret and apply in giving their rulings on particular cases. It is in turn this case law that forms the base for common law. In the commercial sphere laws determine the licensing and regulatory conditions for financial institutions, the procedures for the registration of companies and provision for consumer protection. The statutes do not provide for the terms of particular contracts and their enforcement, which is a matter for the courts and not the statutory authorities to settle in the event of disputes.

As banking and financial contracts are always evolving to meet the changing needs of clients, statutory provision cannot keep up with contractual innovation. The advantage of common law is that it is malleable, as although precedent is followed by the courts when interpreting similar financial contracts, where there is innovation the courts enjoy considerable discretion. In effect they determine new precedents for the innovative contracts that will have implications for future cases. The judiciary itself becomes creative, adjusting to new circumstances through a process of incremental adaptation and change. As there are no national laws governing specific Islamic financial contracts, the interpretation and enforcement of the contracts has been through the courts. It is the judiciary that has taken the initiative and produced what has become the body of common law of relevance to the enforcement of *Shari'ah*-compliant contracts.

Common law and *Shari'ah*

There are many similarities between common law and *Shari'ah* both in terms of methodology and in how the laws are derived. Although the judiciary look to national laws for guidance and the *Shari'ah* scholars look to the Quran and the Hadith, much of their work involves searching for legal precedent, which in the case of *Shari'ah* scholars involves the study of Islamic jurisprudence, *fiqh*, covering the rulings or *fatwa* in previous cases. As with the common law judiciary, where cases are very similar to those subject to previous adjudications, the *Shari'ah* scholars will usually follow precedent, but where there are material differences, they can exercise discretion over what they rule when new *fatwas* are issued. The process of interpretation is described as *ijtihad*, the attempt to derive a just ruling based in the principles of Islamic teaching and assessing whether customary law is appropriate and fair or if it should be modified. Often no modification is required as a general Islamic legal principle is that all acts are permissible unless they are specifically prohibited.

Some legal historians suggest that common law had at least some of its roots in *Shari'ah* as the Normans, the last invaders of England in the Middle Ages, also ruled the island of Sicily. The Normans adopted many Sicilian legal concepts, which were in turn influenced by *Shari'ah*, as geographically Sicily was very close to North Africa and like Spain had been previously under Muslim rule.[2] When the Normans took over Sicily they not only left its legal system largely intact, but found many of the ideas of practical use. Just as with the Crusaders, the interaction between Europe and the Islamic world was a two-way process, with the influence of Islamic ideas and legal concepts spreading to Europe and the territories that were to become the United Kingdom long before the reverse process occurred of civil and common law spreading to the Islamic world as a result of colonialism.

There are many concepts shared by *Shari'ah* and English Common Law, for example, the concept of a binding agreement or covenant which can be equated with the Islamic *aqd*, a legal obligation created by an offer and acceptance, such as the offer of finance in return for accepting the terms of repayment. In English medieval law there was the concept of recent dispossession, an action to recover land of which the plaintiff had been dispossessed. Proving dispossession was sufficient for the legal recognition of the return of the land, rather than proving ownership, which in the absence of the original title documents could prove almost impossible. In *Shari'ah* the concept of *istihqaq* is very similar, although in modern Morocco and Turkey it is now applied to scholarship entitlement based on academic merit, a rather different meaning of the term.

English Common Law often involves trial by jury, with twelve men or women selected from the general public to give their verdict in a criminal trial as to whether the accused is innocent or guilty. In Islamic law there is the concept of *lafif* which also involves appointing a jury of twelve drawn from the neighbourhood in which the crime occurred. By selecting upright and honest citizens to serve on a jury, this increases the confidence of the general public that justice is being done; indeed it means the general public become stakeholders in the justice system. The role of the judge is to guide the jury and determine the appropriate sentence for the wrongdoer, not to determine innocence or guilt.

There are also similarities in the legal training for those administering common law and Islamic law. In common law jurisdictions law schools or colleges of law were often independent of government-funded universities and run by law societies representing the profession. In Islamic legal environments law students attended *madrasah* where they studied *fiqh*, Islamic jurisprudence, by examining the writings and *fatwa* of Islamic scholars down the ages and the reasoning underlying the *fatwa*. *Madrasah* were particularly well established in the Indian sub-continent and central Asia, and were usually attached to mosques, but offered a more specialist legal education and not simply introductory courses in Islamic studies. *Madrasah*, like law schools, were independent of government, but just as state-funded universities in the West play an increasing role in legal education, in the Muslim world there has been a parallel involvement by governments, including in Al Ahzar in Cairo, the oldest seat of Muslim learning and scholarship.

In the field of finance there are important concepts shared by *Shari'ah* and common law, notably *hawala*, a contract involving agency, and *waqf*, which can be regarded as similar to a trust. There was no concept of agency in Roman law but as trans-Mediterranean trade increased in the medieval period *hawala* was used for payments involving Muslim merchants.[3] The terms *aval* in French law and *avallo* in Italian are believed to be derived from *hawala*. It should be noted that *hawala* refers to a type of contract, mostly used today for money transfers, where the money changer or exchange dealer acts as the agent for the client wanting to make the transfer. *Hawala* is used by many of the migrant workers in the Gulf to send remittances to their families in South Asia. In India, Pakistan, Bangladesh and Afghanistan there are large networks of *hawala* agencies which have close relations with the moneychangers of the Gulf. Within hours of remittances being paid in Dubai, Abu Dhabi and other Gulf centres the families of the migrants can collect the funds from the agencies in South Asia. Payments are made on trust long before the funds are actually transferred, with the charge for such speed and convenience being built into the transfer fees.

Waqf is a trust established under Islamic law often as a result of a bequest in a will. The funds must be utilised in accordance with the instructions of the deceased, and may be used to purchase land to build a mosque or educational or other buildings to house *madrasah* or other religious institutions.[4] The establishment of a cash *waqf* is also possible, with the bequest invested in a portfolio of financial assets, the income from which will be used for charitable purposes, including educational scholarships for those with little or no personal wealth. As with a trust under English Common Law, the *waqf* will be administered by trustees who are obliged to ensure that the wishes of the deceased are respected and that the funds are used for charitable purposes in accordance with *Shari'ah*. As *waqf* literally means detention, the trustees' discretion is very limited, the idea being that they are bound by the terms of the trust. *Waqf* have their own legal personality as with trusts under English Common Law, and the trustees should never act in their own material interest, but rather in accordance with the provisions under which the *waqf* was established.

Civil law and *Shari'ah*

Most Muslim-majority states, including all the countries of the Arab world, Iran, Turkey and Indonesia, the most populous Muslim country, are civil- rather than common-law jurisdictions. Civil law derives from Roman law and it was codified during the reign of Napoleon in France and by some of the Germanic states, and is the legal system prevalent in most of continental Europe. It was introduced into Egypt during the period of Napoleon's occupation, and from Egypt spread to most other Arab countries, apart from those in the Maghreb which came directly under French influence and Greater Syria, including Lebanon, which was also much influenced by France.

Civil law recognises the primacy of the state and national legislation, and unlike in common law, the courts cannot make laws and are not bound by precedent. Rather their remit is to interpret and apply state laws. There are no juries, with the ultimate decisions being made by the judge or the panel of judges. The civil legal system is usually described as inquisitorial, the aim being to search for the true facts of any case. In contrast the common-law system is adversarial, with much stress placed on whether the prosecution or the defence has the best legal arguments.

In many respects *Shari'ah* is more compatible with common than civil law given the shared concepts explained in the previous section. In many Muslim-majority countries Islam is referred to in general terms in the constitution, but the laws governing banking and commercial transactions are based on those in other civil-law jurisdictions, and enforcement is through secular rather than *Shari'ah* courts. States can be classified as Islamic because of their constitutions, but what this means in practice is open to debate. Constitutional principles and provisions rarely get applied in the economic and financial sphere, indeed there are no examples where there are any sections or clauses specifying that the banking or financial system should be Islamic, even in Saudi Arabia. Rather what is in some cases specified is that no laws should be enacted which conflict with the teaching of Islam. Some Muslim-majority countries, notably Turkey, have secular constitutions that contain no reference to religion and in Ankara the Constitutional Court ensures that there is no religious input, a position supported by the powerful Turkish military.

In civil-law jurisdictions as the legal parameters are determined by the state the legitimacy arises out of a social contract whereby citizens are entitled to equal treatment under the law. The assumption of civil law is that the state must pass laws and provide a framework for all matters, including financial activity. As civil law does not have provisions for the establishment of trusts, for example, if trusts are required for financial contracts specific laws will have to be enacted to provide for these, as has been the case in Bahrain and Lebanon. Trusts are required for the issuance and trading of Islamic *sukuk* securities as the assets used as backing for the *sukuk* are held in trust on behalf of the investors and the trust administers all payments. The role of trusts in *sukuk* contracts will be explained in Chapter 9.

Civil law is less adaptable to change as legislation has to be passed rather than case law determining precedents. Islamic banking and finance has developed in the United Kingdom without the need for legislative provision, apart from minor changes introduced in the annual finance acts which accompany the budget. In the United Kingdom stamp duty is levied when residential property is purchased and sold. As *murabaha* housing finance involved an Islamic bank purchasing the property and then reselling it to the client, this resulted in double stamp duty. With a conventional mortgage the client obtained a loan from the bank to purchase the property and hence stamp duty was only paid once. As a consequence the tax system discriminated against those seeking Islamic mortgages and made the costs of such mortgages uncompetitive. As a result of lobbying by the Islamic Council of Britain a change to the Finance Act was introduced in April 2003 resulting in only a single stamp duty being levied on 'alternative' mortgages, the designation for Islamic mortgages. The initial exemption for *murabaha*-based mortgages was subsequently extended in later Finance Acts to provide similar exemptions for *ijara*- and *musharaka*-based mortgages, the latter having become the most popular structure.

In contrast to the positive experience in the United Kingdom, attempts to introduce legislation to facilitate Islamic banking and finance in France have proved very difficult. As the United Kingdom is a common-law jurisdiction, no legislative provision was required for the trusts used for *sukuk*. In contrast, in France special legislation was necessary, and although the necessary legislation was approved by the Chambre des Deputies, the French lower house of parliament, the legislation was rejected by the

Senate in 2010 and has yet to be taken forward. As France has the largest Muslim population in Europe, exceeding 5 million, it is unfortunate that Islamic finance has become a political issue because of the need to have special legislation.

Compatibility of the Maliki school of *Shari'ah* with common law

There are four major schools of Sunni jurisprudence, the Hanafi, Hambali, Shafi'i and the Maliki, and in addition the Jafari school, which the majority of Shia follow. All five founders of these schools looked to the Quran and the Hadith as the ultimate sources of Islamic law, and the differences between the schools, especially with regard to Islamic financing issues, should not be exaggerated. The Hambali school, which predominates in Saudi Arabia, is regarded as the purist or strictest as it takes the teaching of the Quran literally and acknowledges no other source of law. The Shafii school, which originated in Medina, predominates in Egypt and the United Arab Emirates, and has the most geographic spread, as it also predominates in Malaysia and Indonesia. It is often regarded as the most liberal, including in matters of finance.

The Malaki school is often regarded as the closest to English Common Law as although its ultimate source of reference is the Quran and the Hadith, it recognises that in particular disputes either of these sources may not provide detailed guidance, or there may be doubts or even confusion about how the Hadith should be interpreted.[5] Therefore, as the Prophet ruled Medina the legal practices of the first three generations of *salaf*, the righteous predecessors, are believed to be extemporary in terms of the living *sunnah*, the practice of Islamic law. As much of the legal practice pre-dated Islam, it was customary law, hence the parallel with common law. It was only those customary laws which were deemed unjust by the followers of the Prophet that were revised, but this did not apply to most traditional laws. In Islam everything is permissible unless it is explicitly forbidden in every sphere including the legal. This meant there was no need to change laws for the sake of change; indeed this would be unnecessary and inappropriate.

Today the Malaki school predominates in most of Northern and Central Africa apart from northern Egypt and the coastal region of East Africa from Somalia to Zanzibar where the Shafi school predominates. Given the developed nature of customary law in most African states it is not surprising that the Malaki school became influential, blending as it does the rich African legal inheritance with respect for the Quran and the Hadith where applicable to particular disputes. In those countries in Africa which adopted English Common Law as a result of being part of the British Empire, customary and *Shari'ah* law coexisted with the laws that were enacted, and there was little interference in the traditional justice system. For trade, commerce and banking, however, English law generally applied, not least because the banks were largely British owned and much trade was with the United Kingdom.

English Common Law rulings on Islamic financial disputes

Most cross-border contracts in Islamic finance are governed by English Common Law. The first litigation heard in the English courts involved the case of the Shamil Bank of Bahrain versus Beximco Pharmaceuticals Limited in 2004.[6] Beximco had obtained trade financing from the Shamil Bank through a *murabaha* contract whereby Beximco agreed to purchase goods from the bank on a deferred payments basis, which previously the bank had purchased on its behalf. The dispute arose when Beximco defaulted on the *murabaha* contract by failing to make the agreed payments, which resulted in the Shamil Bank issuing formal court proceedings by making an application to the High Court in London for a summary judgment.

Beximco's defence lawyers argued that under the governing law clause of the *murabaha* contracts, the finance agreements were enforceable only if they were valid and enforceable both in accordance with the principles of *Shari'ah* and in accordance with English law. Beximco's defence team argued that the contract was not *Shari'ah* compliant as the payments amounted to interest which was prohibited under Islamic law. Therefore there was no justification for the payment being made.

The High Court did not accept the argument that the payments from Beximco could not be enforced. The judges argued that:

> Subject to the principles of the Glorious *Shari'ah*, this Agreement shall be governed by and construed in accordance with the laws of England.

In other words, the agreement could be enforced under English Common Law, as there could only be one law governing the contract. The High Court was not qualified to judge whether the agreement was *Shari'ah* compliant or not, as that was a matter for the *Shari'ah* scholars. However, *Shari'ah* principles were not laws as recognised by the English courts, and therefore the validity of the *murabaha* contract was assessed under English Common Law. Hence, Beximco was judged liable to make the payments stipulated in the contract which its chief executive officer had signed.

Beximco appealed against the judgement by the High

Court, and the Court of Appeal in London examined the High Court's decision and the explanation given by the judge. It subsequently upheld the judgement which has created an important precedent under English Common Law that will be referred to by those involved in future disputes regarding Islamic financial contracts.

The Rome Convention which governs international commercial transactions stipulates that a contract shall be governed by 'the law chosen by the parties' and the reference to a choice of law is to the law of a country, not to a non-national system of law such as *Shari'ah*. Although it is open to the parties to a contract to incorporate some provisions of a foreign law into an English contract, this applies only in cases where the parties have sufficiently identified specific provisions of a foreign law or an international code or set of rules. In the case of Beximco and the Shamil Bank the general reference to principles of *Shari'ah* in the governing law clause did not identify those aspects of *Shari'ah* which were intended to be incorporated into the contract. However, the High Court indicated that had the relevant *Shari'ah* principles been validly incorporated in this case, Beximco might have succeeded in their application.

A more recent disagreement ruling in the case of Investment Dar of Kuwait and Blom Bank of Lebanon also ended up in the High Court in London in 2009.[7] The dispute centred on over $10 million which Blom Bank claimed it was owed by Investment Dar. Blom Bank had originally entered into a *wakala* agreement with Investment Dar, a company that specialised in *Shari'ah*-compliant investment. Under this master contract Investment Dar was to manage the funds invested as *wakeel*, or agent, and from time to time Blom would deposit funds. The agreement provided for the return of the capital invested plus a predetermined return which would be fixed when the funds were placed.

Clause 5.5 was especially important as it gave the *wakeel* power to adjust the anticipated profit originally specified if there was a change of circumstances. In that event the *wakeel* could be required to terminate the *wakala* transaction in which case there was an obligation to pay to the *muwakkil* (depositor) the investment amount, that is, the amount originally invested, together with the original anticipated profit calculated for the investment period that had elapsed. This was an important provision because it was an unconditional obligation to pay in the event of termination the original anticipated profit whether or not it had in fact been earned on the investment. Therefore the contract could not be regarded as a pure agency or trust.

The dispute arose because, due to the fall in the value of its investments during the global financial crisis of 2008, Investment Dar was unable to repay Blom Bank the principal or even the return on the investment. Investment Dar rather surprisingly asserted that it was unwilling to pay because the contract was not *Shari'ah* compliant and the returns on the investment amounted to interest. As the *Shari'ah* board of Investment Dar had already approved the contract, this justification for non-payment seemed inconsistent. As with the Beximco/Shamil Bank case, the High Court did not seek to be involved in *Shari'ah* matters, but Judge Pearle, who heard the case, found in favour of Blom Bank given the wording of the agreement freely entered into by the parties.

English law rulings in Malaysia on Islamic financing contracts

As already indicated, Malaysia adopted an English Common Law system during the colonial period. In recent years its national courts have been asked for rulings on Islamic financial contracts and financial disputes, many of the latter involving inheritance issues, an area subject to much litigation. It is the former which will be considered here, notably the High Court ruling of September 2008 that the application of *Al-Bai' Bithaman Ajil* (BBA), a very popular Islamic home-loan financing contract in Malaysia for the last two decades but much criticised abroad, is contrary to Malaysia's Islamic Banking Act of 1983.

In what became another widely discussed judgement, High Court Judge Datuk Abdul Wahab Patail ruled that the sale element in the BBA is 'not a bona fide sale'. He also brought into question the profit portion of the facility. The judgement has forced Islamic banks and financial institutions to re-examine their legal documentation. The Kuala Lumpur High Court commercial court division examined eleven cases involving Bank Islam Malaysia and the Arab-Malaysian Finance House. The BBA house financing is a contract of deferred payment sale at an agreed selling price, which includes a profit margin agreed on by the customer and the bank. Profit in this context was regarded as justified since it is derived from the buying and selling transaction as opposed to interest accruing from the principal lent.[8]

Abdul Wahab's judgement disagreed with this interpretation of a BBA contract as he challenged its substance. He argued that the sale was not a bona fide sale, but a financing transaction, and the profit portion arising from such BBA transactions rendered the facility contrary to the Islamic Banking Act of 1983 and the Banking and Financial Institutions Act of 1989. In contrast, earlier judges had ruled that there is no dispute, that the concepts of BBA contracts were in principle Islamic in nature since no interest was involved. For Abdul Wahab this was seen as unsatisfactory as it was a question of the Court looking at the particular facts.[9]

In an earlier case in 2006 involving Affin Bank versus Zulkifli Abdullah, the judge passed a ruling on the calculation of the amount to be paid in the event of a foreclosure. Previously banks had calculated the amount owed up to the full period of the facility, even though the borrowers may have defaulted only a few years into the financing. Abdul Wahab wrote that the Court accepted that where the bank is the owner or had become the owner under a novation agreement, the sale to the customer is a bona fide sale, and the selling price is as interpreted in the case of Affin Bank versus Zulkifli Abdullah. In other words, where the bank was the owner of the property, by a direct purchase from the vendor or by a novation from its customer, and then sold the property to the customer, the bank's interpretation of the bank's selling price is rejected and the Court applies the equitable interpretation. Hence the selling price in the event of a foreclosure would be the market valuation at the time. The banks are still appealing against this judgement.[10]

Two conclusions are to be drawn from these Malaysian Court rulings. Firstly, from the Abdul Wahab ruling it is evident that the contracts offered by Islamic banks have not only to be acceptable from a *Shari'ah* perspective but, even more importantly, they must comply with national law. Secondly, from the Affin Bank case it is evident that purchases and sales are legally binding and the prices at which they occur should be equitable and in line with market valuations. Banks cannot impose unjust penalties on defaulters, as not only is this unfair under Islamic teaching, but it also contravenes the principles of English Common Law.

Notes

1. John Esposito, *Islam: the Straight Path*, 3rd edn (Oxford: Oxford University Press, 1998), pp. 87–8.
2. Donald L. Horowitz, 'The Qur'an and the Common Law:

Islamic law reform and the theory of legal change', *American Journal of Comparative Law*, 42: 3, Summer 1994, pp. 543–80.

3. Mohammed El Qorchi, '*Hawala*', *Finance and Development*, 39: 4, pp. 40–6.

4. Timur Kuran, 'The provision of public goods under Islamic law: origins, impact and limitations of the waqf system', *Law and Society Review*, 35: 4, 2001, pp. 841–98.

5. Joseph Schacht, 'Foreign elements in ancient Islamic law', *Journal of Comparative Legislation and International Law*, 32: 3/4, 1950, pp. 9–17.

6. Nicholas H. D. Foster, 'Islamic finance law as an emergent legal system', *Arab Law Quarterly*, 21: 2, 2007, pp. 170–88.

7. Wafica Ali Ghoul, 'The dilemma facing Islamic finance and lessons learnt from the global financial crisis', *Journal of Islamic Economics Banking and Finance*, 7: 1, 2011, pp. 57–76.

8. Angelo M. Venardos, *Islamic Banking and Finance in South East Asia: its Development and Future*, 2nd edn (Singapore: World Scientific Publishing, 2006), pp. 224–5.

9. Saiful Azhar Rosly, '*Shari'ah* parameters reconsidered', *International Journal of Islamic and Middle Eastern Finance and Management*, 3: 2, 2010, pp. 132–46.

10. Ahmad Hidayat Buang, 'Islamic contracts in a secular court setting? Lessons from Malaysia', *Arab Law Quarterly*, 21: 4, 2007, pp. 317–40.

CHAPTER 3
TERMS AND CONDITIONS GOVERNING ISLAMIC BANK DEPOSITS

The aim of this chapter is to explain how the contracts for deposits designated as Islamic differ from those with conventional banks. The structure of different types of *Shari'ah*-compliant deposit contracts is explained including current accounts and *mudaraba* deposits which are the Islamic equivalent of conventional savings deposits. The treasury accounts offered by some Islamic banks are also examined. Examples of the actual accounts offered by leading Islamic banks are discussed.

The legal position regarding both conventional and Islamic deposits is similar, as the deposits represent a liability for the bank but an asset for the depositor. The client is the beneficial owner of the deposit, but not of the bank, which will be owned by its shareholders. The depositors entrust their money to the bank, which in turn has a duty of trust to look after the money and return it in full and in compliance with the terms for withdrawals set out in the deposit contract. In Islamic finance the duty of trust is referred to as *amanah*; hence the name of the Islamic financing subsidiary of HSBC.

Islamic current-account bank deposits

As economies develop and more people are in formal employment they find they need bank accounts. While day labourers were often paid in cash in the past, most employees in salaried occupations have their monthly pay credited to their bank accounts. Often their employment contract stipulates that they must open a bank account as employers seek to streamline their payroll administration by transferring funds electronically rather than handling large amounts of cash. Electronic transfers into bank accounts are more secure for both employers and employees, not least in terms of crime prevention.

Although cash transactions prevailed historically in most Islamic communities, today bank accounts are becoming indispensable. Muslim employees can of course open accounts with conventional banks and have their salaries credited by their employers. As conventional banks will however use their deposits to fund lending on which interest is charged, Muslims would therefore be contributing to *riba*-based financing. As *riba* is forbidden in *Shari'ah*, such deposits would be considered *haram*, unless there was no alternative available, in which case bank customers could argue that on grounds of necessity, they must use such accounts if they are to remain in employment and support their families.[1]

There are obvious advantages of *Shari'ah*-compliant current accounts for pious depositors. Where Islamic banks are already established, or where conventional banks offer *Shari'ah*-compliant deposits and provide an undertaking that these deposits will be not be used for *riba*-based financing, Muslims have the opportunity to open current accounts which can be regarded as *halal*.[2] Of course they will expect the same facilities with such accounts as with conventional deposits, otherwise the argument of necessity could be used by them to continue to maintain their existing current accounts, despite such accounts promoting *riba*.

Often current-account holders with conventional banks earn no interest, or where they earn interest, it is usually minimal. Islamic banks cannot offer interest on any current account, and in most cases provide no alternative financial return. They, however, provide numerous account services to account holders. The Dubai Islamic Bank, for example, offers:

- free cheque book
- free teller transactions
- free Al Islami debit card
- free monthly statements
- free electronic banking (online, land-line phone)
- nominal charges on mobile-phone banking
- free Etisalat (UAE phone company) and utility bill payments.[3]

Most clients find the facility to view their accounts online particularly useful as it enables them to monitor their account credits and debits from their homes and ensure their accounts are in credit. Overdrafts on which conventional banks charge interest are not available from Islamic banks, and therefore ensuring accounts are in credit is especially important, as otherwise debit-card payments and withdrawals will no longer be possible. This could potentially be inconvenient for clients, but on the other hand they have the assurance that they will never be charged interest.

As there is significant migration in the Islamic world, with many Muslim expatriates working in the Gulf in particular, money transfer services for remittances are important.

Although many Muslims working in low-paid manual occupations continue to use money-exchange firms and pay in cash the money to be transferred, those in higher-paid professional occupations use bank transfers rather than having to queue up at money-exchange firms. Many Islamic banks offer online transfer facilities to current-account holders, a modern electronic version of traditional *hawala*, which referred to transfers made through a trusted agent. As there is no manual processing involved, the costs of such transfers are often significantly lower than those of the money-exchange firms, but the recipient of the funds must have a bank account with an International Bank Account Number (IBAN), as well as the sender. As this number enables the Islamic bank of the sender to verify electronically the existence of the account of the recipient to minimise transfer errors, the system is much more secure than those operated manually.

Islamic debit cards

Al Islami debit cards are a better alternative to cash payments as clients do not have to carry large quantities of currency which could be stolen. Also many people prefer to use their own clean debit card for reasons of hygiene rather than soiled currency notes. The debit cards can in any case be used to withdraw cash from the automatic teller machines (ATMs) in bank branches as well as in shopping malls, usually at any time. Cash withdrawal amounts are limited, however, to a specific sum each period, usually from one to three days, in the interests of the security of the client.

Debit cards are of course mainly used for point-of-sale payments in supermarkets, clothes shop and other retail establishments as well as for settling hotel bills. When debit cards are used an electronic record is maintained for every transaction, which enables clients to monitor all their own expenditures, as well as that of other family members who are authorised card users. Expenditure in pubs, liquor stores or betting shops, all of which supply products that are *haram*, can immediately be detected.

There is of course no financing or debt with debit cards, unlike credit cards, as clients are simply withdrawing their own money. Until recently, most Islamic banks issued debit cards rather than credit cards, as interest was payable on outstanding credit-card debt. However, many Islamic banks now issue both to current-account customers, and clients have the option of using either to make payments. The features of Islamic credit cards, and what makes them *Shari'ah* compliant, will be explained in the next chapter which deals with Islamic financing.

The implications of demand deposits

Current accounts are often referred to as demand deposits as clients expect to be able to withdraw their money at any time. This means the banks have to maintain sufficient liquidity to meet all demands for withdrawals, including maintaining adequate cash holdings in bank branches and ATMs. Usually current accounts are very active, often with many transactions being recorded every day, which also increases the need for liquidity by the banks. Hence banks which are dependent on current accounts for most of their deposit liabilities will have to ensure that their assets are sufficiently liquid to meet these demands. As Islamic banks cannot borrow from other banks through inter-bank money markets because such borrowing would incur interest payments, they have to be particularly careful in their management of assets.

Fiqh muamalat pertaining to current accounts

There are three concepts in *fiqh muamalat* which are often applied to Islamic current-account deposits. The first is *qard hasan*, the second is *amanah* or trust, and the third is *daman*, which involves guarantees. *Qard hasan*, or an interest-free loan, is the only type of lending which is permissible under *Shari'ah*. When a client opens a current account, the bank is being given an interest-free loan, but in return the client has the right to ask that the loan is repaid in full, or partially repaid, at any time on demand. Iran's Law on Interest-Free Banking of 1983 refers specifically to *qard hasan* deposits under Article 3 of Chapter 2 on the mobilisation of monetary resources. Under Article 6 the law refers to the incentives which can be used to encourage such deposits. These include:

- non-fixed bonuses, including in cash or in kind;
- exempting depositors from, or granting discounts in, payment of commissions and fees for services;
- according priority to depositors in the use of banking facilities, in particular access to funding.

The practice of providing bonuses has been criticised as current-account depositors are not involved in risk sharing and therefore any profit-sharing reward is unjustified, even though there is a small risk of the bank defaulting on its obligations. However, a counterargument is that the bonus is not a profit share, but rather a gift, or *hiba*, and such returns may be regarded as a necessary incentive in countries such as Iran where the rate of inflation is high. In 2008 the inflation rate peaked at 29 per cent, and even during the 2009 recession it remained at 18.5 per cent.

Hence, as current-account depositors are only guaranteed to get the nominal value of their deposits returned, in terms of purchasing power the value of the amounts withdrawn will be worth significantly less than the original deposits. In other words, the *hiba* is likely to be, at best, a partial compensation.

The concepts of *amanah* and *daman* are both relevant for Islamic current-account deposits as they highlight the characteristics of the contractual relationship between an Islamic bank and its clients. *Amanah* refers to trust, in this case the obligations of the Islamic bank entrusted with the current-account depositor's funds. In particular, the Islamic bank is liable for any breach of contract or negligence in handling the depositor's funds, although this does not necessarily amount to a deposit guarantee. The obligation of an Islamic bank as *daman* is greater, as this is not merely a matter of avoiding negligence, but of guaranteeing to the depositor that they will be able to withdraw funds to the same nominal value as the sums which were deposited, or in other words repay the deposit balance in full on demand.

Mudaraba investment deposits

Clients with surplus funds who want to earn income often open savings accounts on which they receive interest on their credit balances. Islamic banks cannot offer such accounts because of the prohibition on *riba*, as there can be no moral justification for earning a return on virtually risk-free deposits. Islamic banks have developed a variety of accounts which yield a return for clients prepared to share risk, the most popular being investment deposits based on *mudaraba* contracts.[4]

Unrestricted *mudaraba* deposits

Mudaraba is a contract which involves a financier (the *rabb al maal*) and an entrepreneur (the *mudarib*) forming a partnership the purpose of which is to generate profits for both parties through a commercial venture. In the case of unrestricted *mudaraba* investment deposits it is the depositor who is the *rabb al maal* and the bank which serves as *mudarib*. The investment depositor shares in the bank's profit, these profit payments being a *Shari'ah*-compliant alternative to the interest returns paid on a conventional savings account.[5] The designation 'unrestricted' indicates that the bank is free to use the funding for whatever purpose it believes will be profitable, provided it is *Shari'ah* compliant.

Where losses are incurred under *mudaraba*, these are borne by the *rabb al maal* rather than the *mudarib*. The justification for this liability is that the *mudarib* will have no earnings when losses are incurred, despite devoting much time and energy to trying to pursue profitable opportunities. The *raab al maal* in contrast is a more passive partner, so it is felt that they should bear any losses, and as their deposits are of surplus funds not required immediately, they clearly have the capacity to absorb losses.

The value of *mudaraba* deposits therefore cannot be guaranteed unlike deposits in conventional savings accounts or indeed current accounts with Islamic or conventional banks. There is not only the risk of a variable profit payment, but also potential exposure to capital losses, although this is usually mitigated by Islamic banks maintaining profit-equalisation reserves as will be explained later in this chapter. Of course where losses result from negligence or misappropriation of funds by the *mudarib* rather than business risk, the *raab al maal* has the right to litigate against the *mudarib* for the return of the deposited funds.

It is the risk sharing that justifies the profit accruing to the *rabb al maal*. Profits will inevitably vary over time, as these will be a function of both macroeconomic conditions, which will affect the fortunes of the financial sector as a whole, and the performance of the management, which will impact on the profitability of the institutions they manage. The relationship between actual profits and what gets distributed in any business is complex as if too much profit is distributed there may be insufficient retained earnings to finance investment. In other words, large short-term profit distributions could be at the expense of long-term earnings for investors. Although under traditional *mudaraba* contracts the share accruing to the *raab al maal* and the *mudarib* is fixed in advance, and cannot be varied for the duration of the contract, this might result in a degree of inflexibility that might be detrimental for a modern business. Therefore, in practice although the proportions or shares are fixed, the rates for profit distributions are determined both by what is believed will be sustainable and the need to pay a competitive return in order to retain the *mudaraba* depositors.

Profit sharing in practice

The profit distributions paid by Kuveyt Türk are shown in Table 3.1. Kuveyt Türk is a Turkish participation bank which is *Shari'ah* compliant with the Kuwait Finance House as its major shareholder.

The rates shown are only available for deposits of one year or longer. Note that profit payments are highest for deposits denominated in Turkish lira, reflecting inflationary expectations for that currency. Rates are significantly lower for deposits in US dollars, but lowest of all for deposits in euros, reflecting the perceived strengths of the currency and the likelihood of appreciation. Depositors seeking monthly

Table 3.1 *Profit rates paid to investment account depositors with Kuveyt Türk*

Frequency	Turkish lira gross	Turkish lira net	$US gross	$US net	€ gross	€ net
Monthly	8.58	7.29	3.41	2.90	3.47	2.95
Quarterly	8.83	7.51	3.65	3.10	3.56	3.03
Semi annual	9.18	7.80	3.68	3.13	3.61	3.07
Annual	9.60	8.16	3.80	3.25	3.73	3.17

Source: Kuveyt Türk, Istanbul (May 2011), www.kuveytturk.com.tr.

returns receive less than depositors who are content with a single annual return. Gross refers to before-tax and net the after-tax return.

Kuveyt Türk also offers shorter term participation accounts for 30 days or longer based on *mudaraba*, with the returns depending not only on the currency chosen, but also on the minimum amount deposited. For classic accounts that pay the least the minimum sum is €1,000, for silver accounts €50,000, for gold €100,000, for platinum €250,000 and for platinum plus €800,000. Amounts distributed also depend on the period for the deposit, as with conventional time deposits, those for 270 days enjoying a higher profit share than those for only 30 days.

Some Islamic banks have even more steeply tiered profit rates depending on the period of notice or the length of the fixed term. Those for Islamic Bank of Britain for sterling deposits are illustrated in Table 3.2. Deposits with a period of notice for withdrawal are distinguished from time deposits which must be held to maturity to earn the advertised return, maturity ranging from three to twenty-four months. The corresponding deposits for Dubai Islamic Bank are also shown in Table 3.2, these being for dirham-denominated deposits. As the US dollar, to which the UAE dirham is fixed,

Table 3.2 *Islamic Bank of Britain (IBB) and Dubai Islamic Bank (DIB) profit rates*

Deposit type	IBB return %	DIB return %
On-demand savings	0.05	0.75
60-day notice	1.00	N/A
Fixed term 1 month	N/A	2.05
Fixed term 3 months	0.10	2.10
Fixed term 6 months	1.25	2.15
Fixed term 12 months	1.50	2.25
Fixed term 18 months	1.75	N/A
Fixed term 24 months	2.00	N/A

Source: IBB, London, www.islamic-bank.com and DIB, www.alislami.ae (May 2011).

is expected to depreciate against Asian currencies and the euro, depositors expect higher payouts for all time periods.

Profit-equalisation reserves and *mudaraba* depositor rights

In order to retain flexibility to make profit distributions to investors in *mudaraba* accounts in line with market expectations most Islamic banks retain a profit-equalisation reserve. In years when profits are high, rather than distributing excessive amounts to the *mudaraba* investment depositors, some profits are retained, so that payouts can continue to be made if the bank makes low profits or losses. In the case of the latter the reserves can be drawn on rather than writing down the value of *mudaraba* investment-account balances which would be unpopular with depositors.[6]

It is important to stress that *mudaraba* investment depositors are not shareholders and have no ownership rights over the Islamic bank accepting their deposits. Unlike the shareholders they cannot attend the annual general meetings or exercise voting rights. However, the risks associated with ownership are much greater than those borne by *mudaraba* depositors, as there is a high probability that the value of their shareholdings will decline, whereas thanks to the profit-equalisation reserve, the nominal value of *mudaraba* investment deposits can be maintained. The shareholders are of course hoping for capital gains whereas there is no similar upside for the *mudaraba* depositors who can simply hope to have their capital returned and in the meantime benefit from regular profit-sharing distributions.

There are potential conflicts of interest between shareholders and *mudaraba* investment-account holders with Islamic banks. If higher dividends are paid to shareholders there will be less profit available to distribute to *mudaraba* account holders. The board of directors ultimately represents the interest of the shareholders as owners, and not the *mudaraba* account holders, who are simply depositors, although admittedly with some interest in bank performance that determines their remuneration in the long run.

The market itself helps protect the interests of *mudaraba* investment depositors however, as if profit shares are too low because of high dividend payments, depositors may choose to withdraw their funds. If the deposit base shrinks and hence financing activity, this will reduce the dividends paid to shareholders, and perhaps impact negatively on share prices. In other words, maximising short-term dividends at the expense of the *mudaraba* investment depositors will negatively impact on the longer-term shareholder interests.

Restricted *mudaraba* investment accounts

Deposits in restricted *mudaraba* investment accounts are not utilised by the bank for its own financing, but instead flow through to finance specified projects or businesses. Jordan Islamic Bank pioneered this type of deposit which it describes as:

> deposits received by the Bank from persons desiring to appoint the bank as agent for investing these deposits in a specific project or in a specific manner on the basis that the Bank will receive part of the net profits realised, but without liability for any loss which is not attributed to any violation or fault by the Bank.[7]

The key difference with these restricted deposits is that the bank and the *mudaraba* investment depositor share in the profit from the project rather than sharing in the bank's profit. There are three parties to the contract, the depositor, the bank and the end user of the funds, whereas unrestricted deposits only involve a contract between the depositor and the bank. Note that as with unrestricted accounts it is the depositor who is the *raab al maal* and who bears any losses. Hence the value of these deposits cannot be guaranteed. Nevertheless depositors expect to be able to withdraw, subject to a period of notice, all the sums they deposited and in practice there have been no cases of capital losses. Any liability by the bank for losses is confined to cases of negligence resulting in breaches of contract.

Because deposits in a restricted *mudaraba* account are assigned to a particular company rather than an Islamic bank, there will be a higher risk of losses and greater variability of returns. An Islamic bank can be regarded as a portfolio investor with a wide range of assets the profits from which are shared by the unrestricted *mudaraba* account holders. In contrast, restricted *mudaraba* accounts involve investment concentration, hence the higher risk. Restricted *mudaraba* depositors will, however, accept the higher risk in the expectation of obtaining an enhanced return.

For the company obtaining such financing, the attraction may be the ability to access a further source of financing but without taking on additional equity which could dilute the shareholdings of the existing owners. The restricted *mudaraba* funding also enables the company to avoid the fixed-payments obligations associated with debt financing. Instead it will share its profits, but if there are no profits there will be no obligation to continue to make service payments. The company will nevertheless still have an obligation to pay the restricted *mudaraba* account holders should profits recover.

If the *mudarib* is a sole proprietor then any losses in the event of insolvency would have to be borne by the restricted-investment depositors. Where the business has obtained additional finance from Islamic banks through *murabaha*, *ijara* or other financing facilities, these claims would have to be met first before any remaining sums from asset sales are used to compensate the restricted *mudaraba* investors. However, if the business has private equity shareholders, or is a listed company, the claims of the restricted *mudaraba* depositors would take precedent over those of the ordinary shareholders. Their position in the pecking order is, in other words, similar to preference shareholders, although of course the two types of financing are quite distinctive. Specifically, restricted *mudaraba* depositors expect to have their capital returned at the end of the period, whereas often preference shares convert to common stockholdings.

Restricted *mudaraba* deposits should be regarded as long-term committed capital as there is usually a minimum period of one year before depositors can withdraw their funds. This means restricted *mudaraba* deposits are less liquid than those in current accounts or most deposits in unrestricted *mudaraba* accounts. Hence restricted *mudaraba* accounts are long-term time deposits, with the onus on the client to ask to have their money returned, rather than the deposit maturing and the money being automatically refunded as with short-term treasury deposits. Exit is however guaranteed, and in this sense restricted *mudaraba* accounts are very different to investments in *Shari'ah*-compliant private equity, which is discussed in Chapter 12.

As restricted-investment accounts generate fee income for the Islamic banks, but without an obligation by the bank to repay the deposits, the latter's liabilities, and the assets in which the deposits are invested, can be moved off the bank's balance sheet. This is provided for in the standards of the Accounting and Auditing Organization for Islamic Financial Institutions (AAOIFI) as discussed in Chapter 18 on financial reporting issues.

Islamic treasury deposits

For companies and individuals of high net worth some Islamic banks, including Islamic Bank of Britain, offer treasury deposits. These are suitable for those having large cash holdings, but who are prepared to sacrifice some liquidity in order to get a return. Conventional banks offer treasury accounts paying interest, but Islamic banks cannot do this and instead pay a permissible profit rate. As is the case with other Islamic bank accounts treasury deposits cannot be used to finance interest-based loans. Instead the funds are used for *Shari'ah*-based methods of financing such as *murabaha*, *ijara* and *istisna'a*. In the case of conventional banks offering Islamic treasury deposits, they must be segregated from other *Shari'ah* non-compliant funds.

Usually with treasury accounts depositors expect to get their money refunded in full at the end of the period, which implies a capital guarantee, as is the case with current accounts. Such guarantees cannot be provided for *mudaraba* accounts where it is the risk to the capital which partially justifies the return. For treasury accounts *mudaraba* contracts are therefore not used, but rather *wakala* and *murabaha* contracts.

Wakala *treasury deposits*

These are offered by Islamic Bank of Britain to depositors with at least £50,000 to invest or the equivalent amount in euros or US dollars. *Wakala* is an agency agreement between the client and the bank whereby the bank serves as an agent by investing the sum deposited on behalf of the client. The bank charges an arrangement fee which represents its return on the transaction. The deposit is for a predetermined number of days, and no early or part withdrawals are permitted.[8]

Before the funds are deposited a target profit is negotiated between the bank and the client, this being referred to as the expected profit rate. The rate has to be achievable for the contract to be viable, and in line with market expectations. The agreement states the number of days over which the target profit rate is expected to be achieved, usually 90 or 180 days. Any excess profit over the target rate accrues to the bank, but note that this is very different to a *mudaraba* profit-sharing agreement based on fixed proportions, as any proportion the bank receives is a residual and may vary considerably. The bank's guaranteed return is the arrangement fee, not the excess profit which can be regarded as a performance bonus that is not shared.

The client's profit earnings are protected under the *wakala* agreement, as if the actual profit rate goes below the target, Islamic Bank of Britain will immediately refund the client's deposit in full, plus the profit accruing up to the day the agreement is terminated. If the target profit rate is achieved throughout the period the deposit will only be refunded on maturity, at which point the entire profit payment will be made. In other words, the risk to the client is that the deposit will be refunded prior to maturity, and that they will have to find some other means of getting a return on their funds, or re-deposit with Islamic Bank of Britain at a lower agreed profit rate. The capital is safe, however, and the target profit rate stipulated in the original contract will be honoured, but for a shorter period.

Murabaha *treasury deposits*

For clients with at least £100,000 to deposit, Islamic Bank of Britain offers *murabaha* treasury accounts. As with the *wakala* accounts and most conventional treasury accounts, the client will have to open a current account with the bank, from which sums can be transferred to the *murabaha* account. This account will also be used for repayments of principal and the payment of profits to the client.

Murabaha treasury deposits are accepted for periods from one to sixty months with no withdrawals permissible, even part withdrawals, prior to the agreed maturity date. A profit rate is agreed with the client in advance, with higher rates available for those with at least £250,000 to deposit, reflecting the lower relative transactions costs in processing and managing larger transactions. The funds received through the *murahaba* account are used to purchase commodities, usually on the London Metal Exchange. At the time of purchase the bank, acting as the depositor's agent, will ask its broker to sell the commodity at a predetermined price on a fixed date in the future which corresponds to the deposit maturity. As the selling price is higher than the purchase price the trading transactions will generate a profit which will accrue to the client. The bank charges transaction fees for serving as the buying and selling agent, with these fees agreed in advance.

It should be noted that *murabaha* involves real transactions, and the client will own the commodities from the purchase date to the sale date. The client can opt to take physical delivery of the commodities, but in most cases will simply acquire ownership title, and entrust the commodities to a depository for safe keeping. As the documentation consists of standardised templates legal costs for the bank are modest and are covered from the transactions fee paid by the client. The bank also indemnifies the client against fraud and will ensure the commodities are correctly specified and their value is not impaired.

From a clients perspective the advantage of the *murabaha* treasury deposit is that they have a guarantee to get their deposit refunded in full and the profit is known in advance. The disadvantage is that the commodity transaction involves real costs, including brokerage fees, which increase the fees charged by the bank. The substantial minimum deposit required is because it is not worthwhile to incur these transaction costs for smaller trading operations.

Many clients are attracted to *murabaha* treasury accounts because of the high levels of transparency, as they are informed about the commodities bought and sold, as well as the prices. As physical commodities are involved this gives assurance of the tangible nature of the transaction. In contrast with *wakala* treasury deposits the bank, as agent, can invest the funds at its discretion, with only basic financial information being communicated to the client on the arrangement fee and the profit rate.

Implications of Islamic deposits for the money supply

As bank deposits are used as a substitute for cash holdings they count as part of the money supply, indeed given the convenience of debit-card payments, current-account deposits account for most of the money supply in modern economies. The value of Islamic bank deposits in current accounts counts as equivalent to deposits in conventional accounts when calculating the size of the money supply and its growth. Normally narrow money (M1) represents the sum of currency issued in an economy plus the amount of demand deposits. When central banks compile the statistics for M1, they will usually count demand or current-account deposits with Islamic banks and designated *Shari'ah*-compliant current accounts with conventional banks as part of the total.

Money serves as a medium of exchange, a unit of account and a store of value. Demand deposits with Islamic banks serve all three of these functions, with the exchange function working through the use of debit cards and cheques, the unit of account being the measure of how much is in the account and the store of value function being the ability of depositors to withdraw their deposits in part or in full on demand.

Although the treatment of Islamic demand deposits from a monetary perspective is straightforward, the position of unrestricted and restricted *mudaraba* accounts is more complex, as is the treatment of *wakala* and *murabaha* treasury deposits. Some argue that these should be treated in the same way as savings accounts with conventional banks, which are designated as near money (M2). The components of near money are clearly less liquid than demand deposits as either the deposits are for fixed time periods or subject to periods of notice of withdrawal.

In most cases payments to third parties will not be made directly from *mudaraba*, *wakala* or *murabaha* accounts, but rather the funds transferred, usually electronically through an internet banking facility on a computer or mobile phone, into an Islamic current account from which payments will be made. Hence, money in *mudaraba*, *wakala* or *murabaha* accounts does not usually serve as a unit of exchange. The store of value function can also be questioned in the case of unrestricted and restricted *mudaraba* deposits, as the value of these deposits cannot be guaranteed under *Shari'ah*. With *wakala* and *murabaha* treasury accounts the position is simpler, as the value of these deposits is guaranteed, and therefore they can be regarded as a store of value.

It can be argued that unrestricted and restricted *mudaraba* deposits should be treated differently from a money supply perspective. In particular, many regard restricted *mudaraba* accounts as similar to equity investment, as the downside risks are considerable. As the financier or *rabb al maal*, the depositor will be expected to absorb any losses. If losses are limited this might simply mean forgoing a return. If, however, losses are more substantial the value of the deposit may be written down. Treating deposits with such characteristics as near money is certainly questionable, not least as the funds are tied in for at least one year so they are less liquid than equity investments in stock-exchange-listed companies. Indeed restricted *mudaraba* deposits have some of the characteristics of private equity investments, which nobody would classify as near money.

Summary of Islamic deposit facilities

Table 3.3 *Characteristics of Islamic deposits compared*

Account type	Principal guarantee	Return guarantee	Profit	Minimum period of notice
Current	Yes	No return	None	None
Unrestricted *mudaraba*	No	No	Proportionate	30 days
Restricted *mudaraba*	No	No	Proportionate	One year
Wakala treasury	Yes	Yes	Fixed	90 days
Murabaha treasury	Yes	Yes	Fixed	30 days

Notes

1. Saad A. Metawa and Mohammed Almossawi, 'Banking behaviour of Islamic bank customers: perspectives and implications', *International Journal of Bank Marketing*, 16: 7, 1998, pp. 299–313.

2. Cengiz Erol and Radi El-Bdour, 'Attitudes, behaviour and patronage factors of bank customers towards Islamic banks', *International Journal of Bank Marketing*, 7: 6, 1989, pp. 31–7.

3. www.dib.ae/en/personalbanking_accounts.htm.

4. Hans Visser, *Islamic Finance: Principles and Practice* (Cheltenham, Edward Elgar, 2009), pp. 81–92.

5. Erna Rachmawatı and Ekki Syamsulhakim, *Factors Affecting Mudaraba Deposits in Indonesia*, Working Paper No. 4 in Economics and Development Studies, (Department of Economics, Padjadjaran University, 2004), pp. 1–9.

6. V. Sundararajan, 'Issues in managing profit equalisation reserves and investment risk reserves in Islamic Banks', *Journal of Islamic Economics Banking and Finance*, 4: 1, 2008, pp. 1–12.

7. www.jordanislamicbank.com/accepting_deposits.html.

8. www.islamic-bank.com/personal-banking/savings-products/wakala-treasury-deposit-account/.

CHAPTER 4

CONTRACTS FOR ISLAMIC FINANCING

There are a wide variety of financing facilities provided by Islamic banks compared with conventional banks that concentrate on interest-based loans. Islamic banks can tailor financing to customer requirements and arguably provide a greater choice for their clients. Furthermore, none of the trade-based *murabaha*, *ijara* leasing contracts and *musharaka* participatory financing is available from conventional banks unless they have established Islamic subsidiaries or affiliates. All Islamic financing contracts involve a degree of risk sharing as this justifies the bank's return. This contrasts with conventional loans where the risk is transferred to and entirely borne by the borrower. Islamic bank clients welcome the partial risk relief that comes with participatory finance, and it reduces the likelihood of default.

Nevertheless, lawyers have to consider worst-case scenarios and therefore it is important that Islamic financing contracts include provision for contingencies such as what happens if defaults occur, including the specification of the jurisdiction in which disputes can be resolved. As indicated in Chapter 1, in Islamic law there is much stress on avoiding contractual uncertainty which is regarded as *gharar*. Therefore financing contracts should be carefully drafted and be as specific as possible. The scholars serving on the *Shari'ah* board of the Islamic financial institution will want to assure themselves that there is no ambiguity in the contracts which could result in one of the parties being deceived or unjustly exploited, or indeed both.

Many Islamic financing contracts are to finance the purchase or fund the use of physical goods or commodities or particular services. Islamic financing seldom involves general lines of credit for unspecified purposes. Hence, the Islamic financial institution takes an interest in how the financing is used, a matter that is also of concern to the *Shari'ah*-board members who review and appraise the contracts and who will only permit the funding of transactions involving *halal* goods and services. What is being financed is therefore specified in the contracts.

Murabaha purchase and sale contracts

Islamic finance took off in the 1970s in the Gulf with the establishment of institutions such as Dubai Islamic Bank in 1975 and Kuwait Finance House in 1977. As both Dubai and Kuwait were commercial centres it was inevitable that much of the financing required would be for trade, especially imports. Merchants required finance as they had to pay for imports before the goods could be sold on. *Murabaha* proved the most suitable Islamic contract to cover such financing. Today the contract is also offered as a retail-banking product to finance the purchase of vehicles and household equipment.[1]

A *murabaha* contract is normally entered into by an Islamic bank and a merchant in the case of commercial banking or a personal client in the case of retail banking. It is sometimes referred to as a transactional contract, as it covers an agreed transaction. It is also described as a 'cost plus sale' as the bank purchases the good or commodity for a fixed cost and then sells it on to the client at a higher price, which is referred to as the markup. As most Islamic banks are corporate entities with shareholders and depositors expecting financial returns, they need to generate profits from their financing. The markup for the sale transaction should therefore be regarded as a profit rate. The actual rate will be determined by market competition, or in other words what other banks, conventional as well as Islamic, are charging for finance. This is why Islamic banks are sometimes criticised for charging the same or even more for financing, but the reality is that as price takers rather than price makers they have little choice if they are to be sustainable and remain in business in the long run.

Usually for trade, finance exporters, or the exporter's bank, will require a letter of credit from the importer's bank as a payments guarantee. The cost of this letter of credit will be charged to the importer. With *murabaha*, as it is the importers bank which is making the purchase, not the client, the demand for a letter of credit may be waived. The risk is the credit rating of the bank, not the rating of the client, and as banks will generally be more highly rated than import businesses, guarantees will not be required. This is especially the case for recurrent transactions, where there are often long-standing correspondence relations between the importer's and exporter's banks. Hence, if letters of credit are not required, this makes the total cost of the *murabaha* financing potentially more competitive than that of conventional trade finance. This is one of the factors explaining the increasing popularity of Islamic trade finance in the Gulf from the 1970s, as not only was it *Shari'ah* compliant, but it was also often cheaper.

Cost of *murabaha* financing

In a *murabaha* contract the sale price is predetermined and is specified in the contract between the client and the Islamic bank. The purchase price will be determined by the negotiation between the supplier and the Islamic bank, and will therefore not necessarily be disclosed in the *murabaha* contract. In some jurisdictions, such as the United Kingdom, consumer protection legislation makes it obligatory for all banks, including Islamic banks, to disclose the cost of the finance in terms of the Annual Percentage Rate (APR). There is no requirement of this type in the countries of the Gulf Cooperation Council (GCC), Malaysia or Indonesia but many Islamic banks voluntarily disclose their profit rates. For example, Table 4.1 shows the profit rates quoted to clients by Dubai Islamic Bank.

The profit rates are related to the risks involved with the financing. For home finance the property is usually viewed as a secure asset and good quality collateral. Personal financing rates are low, as this is only offered to clients who have their monthly salaries paid into the bank. Vehicle financing is also low cost as usually an Islamic bank will bulk purchase hundreds of vehicles rather than buying one for a single client.[2] With bulk purchase substantial discounts can be obtained which can enhance the bank's profits on *murabaha* transactions, but as the rates indicate, some of the benefit is passed onto the customer. For small businesses the profit rates charged are higher, as although it is economically and socially desirable to support such enterprises, the reality is that the risk of default is greater as there are many business failures.

The range of profit rates quoted for a particular category of financing reflects the creditworthiness of each customer, as Islamic banks, like their conventional counterparts, use

Table 4.1 *Dubai Islamic Bank profit rates*

Type of finance	Profit rate, %	Processing fee
Home	6.38–11.25	1.25% of financing amount
Personal	5.95–11.00	400 dirham, US$ 109
Vehicle	4.50–10.00	400 dirham, US$ 109
Small business	11.00–13.50	1.5% of financing amount

Source: Dubai Islamic Bank (May 2011).

credit scoring. Those who have been in secure well-paid employment for a number of years and own their own property are able to secure lower rates than the self-employed living in rental property. For home financing, the profit rate offered will also depend on the size of deposit the client is able to pay, with those paying an initial 20 per cent of the value of the property being offered a lower rate than those only able to afford a 10 per cent deposit.

Transactional relationships in *murabaha* contracts

The flow chart in Figure 4.1 shows the relationships between the parties in a *murabaha* transaction. Unless there are recurrent transactions, the contract between the Islamic bank and the client will normally be signed before the Islamic bank makes the purchase from the supplier. This provides assurance to the bank that the client actually wants the good as the bank would not want to make a purchase without being able to sell. This is especially the case if the goods are made to a particular specification of the client, as it may be difficult to find an alternative buyer.

It should be noted that there are two contracts for most *murabaha* transactions, that between the bank and the supplier, and that between the bank and the client. The latter will usually refer to the former, as it is necessary to specify

Figure 4.1 Murabaha *transaction flows*

precisely what goods are being financed to avoid *gharar* or contractual uncertainty. Both contracts may run concurrently from the start but once the advance payment is made by the bank to the supplier and the title is transferred the contract with the supplier is completed. The Islamic bank will not want to take delivery of the goods, which will be transferred directly to the client.

The contract between the Islamic bank and the client may run for one year or more depending on the terms of the deferred payments and the title transfer. The title can be transferred to the client as soon as it is received by the Islamic bank or when the final payment is made. The motivation for an immediate transfer from the bank is that the ownership responsibilities pass directly to the client. Even though the Islamic bank has no ongoing ownership responsibilities it still retains purchaser and seller responsibilities. Hence it is not merely a passive financier. Indeed, it is these responsibilities that justify its markup or profit on the ansaction from a *Shari'ah* perspective.

If the bank transfers the title at the end of the period and retains ownership until then, it will be in a stronger position if there is a client default as it can prevent further usufruct by the client, if necessary by taking a court order to seize the goods. This provides a powerful deterrent against defaulting, and may serve as an inducement to clients to enter discussions with the bank if they are in payment difficulties rather than breaking the relationship. The bank may nevertheless lose financially in the event of a default, as it may be difficult to identify another customer for the goods, which will now be second-hand rather than new. Where the bank passes on the title on day one rather than at the end of the contract period, it will normally take a legal charge over the goods. This means that its financial claims are given precedent over those of other parties that the client may be indebted to. In the case of land and property such charges are recorded by the land registry.

The need for transferable warranties in *murabaha* transactions

With the purchase of vehicles and equipment warranties are usually provided which guarantee that the product will be fit for purpose for a two- or three-year period or even longer. Under the terms of the warranty agreements defective equipment is usually replaced or repaired free of charge. The warranties can be included in the purchase agreement or be subject to a separate agreement, the latter more often applying where extended warranties have been separately purchased, with the cover being provided by an insurance company or *takaful* operator in the case of Islamic finance. However, at present few *takaful* operators provide this type of cover, which involves product knowledge and specialist risk appraisal.

Warranties are usually transferable from the original purchaser, the Islamic bank in the case of a *murabaha* contract, to the end user, the Islamic bank client. If the warranties were not transferable, this would make *murabaha* contract unattractive for the client compared to conventional financing where the client is the first purchaser. To ensure the client does not face such uncertainty and potentially high repair or replacement costs, the Islamic bank will need to ascertain that the warranties are indeed transferable. The *murabaha* contract between the bank and the client may have a clause referring to warranties, but it should be noted that it is the supplier who provides the warranty, not the Islamic bank. The latter's role is confined to acting on behalf of the client and providing due diligence with respect to the contractual obligations of the supplier.

Consumer finance using *murabaha*

In the 1970s and 1980s most *murabaha* finance was for businesses, especially import distributors, as already indicated. As retail banking started to grow throughout the Islamic world from the 1990s, personal financing started to grow at a faster pace than business finance. Many middle-class Muslims earning salaries wanted finance for vehicle and housing purchases, especially in the Gulf and Malaysia, although elsewhere from Morocco and Egypt to Pakistan and Indonesia the demand for Islamic personal finance has started to take off and become one of the most vibrant areas of Islamic banking. Hitherto it was the more affluent, with significant financial assets, who could afford to pay outright for vehicles that accounted for much of the market. However, as mass consumption in the Gulf increased, many could only afford to pay a deposit for a vehicle and required financing, with the deferred payments for the financing being covered from their monthly salaries.

Murabaha proved to be the most popular contract for vehicle financing, with clients paying deposits of one quarter or one tenth of the total financing cost of the vehicle, including the Islamic bank's profit margin, and paying the remainder over thirty-six months of deferred payments, or in some cases as long as sixty months. Rather than simply purchase one vehicle for a particular client, Islamic banks such as Kuwait Finance House (KFH), would purchase 1,000 vehicles and negotiate significant discounts with the manufacturers. Some of this discount could be passed on to the clients, and a portion would contribute to the bank profits for the transactions. As this business increased, KFH acquired its own vehicle showrooms which clients could visit to choose a vehicle from a variety of different manufacturers and models. Indeed, many were attracted to the showrooms primarily by the choice of vehicles rather than the Islamic financing. Choice was more restrictive if using the franchise dealers for a particular make of vehicle. They could also drive away the vehicle subject to credit checks, rather than waiting several months for delivery as is often the case with franchise dealers. The disadvantage is that the client has to choose from the vehicles in stock rather than ordering to their own specifications. However, KFH can provide finance for vehicles purchased from franchise dealers as well as for vehicles purchased from its own showrooms in Shuwaikh.[3]

Second-hand vehicles are also available for purchase as well as new vehicles. Similar terms and conditions apply for the purchase of boats, as sailing and fishing are popular pastimes in Kuwait. The benefits of purchasing a vehicle through KFH are listed in Table 4.2.

For housing finance, local citizens in countries such as Saudi Arabia were entitled to interest-free loans from the government-owned Real Estate Development Corporation, but as demand increased, the waiting list for financing lengthened, as the Corporation had limited funds available. Rather than waiting six or even eight years for housing finance, clients turned to Islamic banks such as Al Rajhi as a source of financing. Al Rajhi provides long-term finance using a *murabaha* structure for owner-occupied housing, acquisition of building land and investment property which

Table 4.2 *Benefits of car purchase from Kuwait Finance House*

- One destination to buy a new car from a variety of vehicles of different makes and models from renowned local car dealerships
- A full range of *Sharia'ah*-compliant financial solutions and services
- Clear purchase and selling prices, instalment period and fixed profit margin
- Competitive prices for a wide variety of vehicles
- KFH representatives are present at most car dealers' showrooms in Kuwait to finalise the selling translations in one place
- Dealership warranty on all vehicles
- Salary transfer to KFH is not required (credit terms and conditions apply)
- A guarantor is not required (credit terms and conditions apply)
- Fast processing and immediate approval of the transaction that fulfils the credit terms and conditions
- Dedicated section for ladies

Source: Kuwait Finance House (June 2011).[4]

is rented by Saudi Arabian citizens to expatriate workers. The amounts of financing that can be obtained in relation to salary levels are shown in Table 4.3 together with the monthly payments. For married couples, where the wife is also a salary earner, which is increasingly common amongst middle-class Saudis, the salaries can be aggregated for the calculation of the amount of financing which can be obtained.

Tawarruq personal and family finance

Many bank clients want personal loans which provide cash rather than finance which is earmarked for a particular purpose as with *murabaha*. The cash can be used to enhance

Table 4.3 *Credit limits and payments for housing finance from Al Rajhi Bank*

Monthly salary	20 Years[a]	25 Years[b]	Monthly payment
SR 5,000	SR 290,000	SR 370,000	SR 2,250
SR 7,500	SR 440,000	SR 560,000	SR 3,400
SR 10,000	SR 580,000	SR 745,000	SR 4,500
SR 12,500	SR 725,000	SR 925,000	SR 5,600
SR 15,000	SR 875,000	SR 1,115,000	SR 6,750

SR = $US 3.75
[a] The finance rate is 4.25% for 20 years; the rate is fixed. The figures are approximate.
[b] The finance rate is 3.25% for 25 years, fixed for first 5 years, then reviewed every 3 years. The figures are approximate.
Source: Al Rajhi Bank (June 2011).[5]

discretionary purchasing power, and provide recipients with resources that they can use if they decide on the spur of the moment to make a purchase which was unplanned. Furthermore, some bank clients may be looking for funding to pay off existing debts, including those to conventional banks. Although Islamic banks do not want to be indirectly supplying funding to pay off loans involving *riba*, if a client is doing this because of a desire to convert all of his or her finance to being *Shari'ah* compliant, it would be inappropriate to obstruct this. In addition, it is worth stressing that if clients cannot obtain cash advances from Islamic banks, some may continue to use conventional interest-based overdrafts and personal loans.

In order to provide cash advances Islamic banks in the Gulf enhanced the *murabaha* contract by buying back from the client the goods acquired through a standard *murabaha* transaction. This contract is referred to as *tawarruq*, literally the monetisation of a trading transaction, also known as reverse *murabaha*. The structure is shown in Figure 4.2,

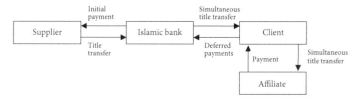

Figure 4.2 *The structure of* tawarruq

which is identical to the flow chart for *murabaha*, but with a simultaneous transfer of title on day one to the client, so that it can be sold on to a third party, the affiliate of the bank, who pays the cash that the client seeks. In other words, the net effect is the same as a conventional loan, with the client making deferred payments in return for a cash advance. In both cases the value of the deferred payments will exceed the amount of the cash advance; this excess is interest in the case of a conventional loan, but represents a profit markup in the case of *tawarruq*.[6]

There are two main objections to *tawarruq* by *Shari'ah* scholars. Firstly, as the same commodity is often traded many times the trading becomes a mere device as the client does not actually want the commodity. Secondly, the transaction becomes meaningless if the bank which originally acquired the commodity buys it back again, as in substance nothing has changed. The *Fiqh* Academy of the Organisation of Islamic Cooperation therefore prohibited *tawarruq* at their meeting in Sharjah in May 2009 declaring:

> to ensure that Islamic banking and financial institutions adopt investment and financing techniques that are *shari'ah*-compliant in all its activities, they should avoid all dubious and prohibited financial techniques, in order to conform to *shari'ah* rules and so that the techniques will ensure the actualization of the *shari'ah* objectives (*maqasid shari'ah*).

Furthermore, it will also ensure the progress and actualization of the socioeconomic objectives of the Muslim world. If the current situation is not rectified, the Muslim world would continue to face serious challenges and economic imbalances that will never end.[7]

In other words, *tawarruq* is seen as dubious and potentially deceitful, in effect a subterfuge, as with this contract an Islamic bank is pretending to undertake trading activity, when in effect it is merely lending. There are in any case alternatives to *tawarruq* for many of the purposes for which it is used. *Murabaha* financing cannot only be used for physical commodities and goods, but also for payments for services. *Tawarruq* is used, for example, to pay for wedding receptions, private medical expenses and even overseas university fees. These are usually one-off rather than continuing payments, which can create short-term financial strain, but which are affordable in the longer term by many from recurrent income. Rather than the client making payments directly using cash obtained through *tawarruq*, the bank can be invoiced directly by the service provider, settle the bill and collect deferred payments from the client. Hence the client does not handle the money.

The merit of such *murabaha* service transactions is that they are for planned expenditures agreed by the client and the bank, whereas *tawarruq* is open to abuse if the client receives cash that they can spend on whatever they want, potentially in a frivolous manner. With *murabaha* there is accountability, but this is not the case with *tawarruq* where the client has complete discretion to pursue their own perceived interest, often without any consultation with their families who may end up being indebted. While it is not the role of Islamic banks to serve as moral guardians for their clients, there is an ethos of social responsibility, which means that the contracts offered should be structured to minimise the possibility of abuse.

Salam contracts

Historically *salam* was used extensively in the Muslim world for the finance of agricultural production. It involves the financier paying in full in advance for a commodity such as wheat or rice to be delivered at a future date, normally three or six months after the payment is made. The advance payment is used by the farmer to cover the costs of seeds, fertilisers and irrigation as well as the wages of the agricultural labourers. This provides for greater flexibility than *murabaha* from the point of view of the farmer, as seed and fertiliser costs can vary and it is often difficult to assess exact labour requirements and therefore the wage bill. However, the purpose of the contract is to facilitate production and a meaningful trading transaction, unlike *tawarruq*. From a *Shari'ah* perspective, and indeed as far as the financier is concerned, it is important to specify exactly in the contract the quantity being supplied and the quality. This ensures there is no *gharar* or contractual uncertainty. *Salam* cannot be used for food items such as fish which have yet to be caught or wild birds, as the suppliers may not be able to meet their contractual obligations if fish stocks prove a problem or if the birds migrate before being caught. Sheep or poultry can, however, be covered as these are already in the possession of the farmer.

The financier will not normally want to take delivery of the agricultural commodity, and therefore a parallel *salam* contract is used to sell the commodity to a wholesaler. Usually the Islamic bank will have already agreed with a wholesaler or client or group of wholesalers the terms of the parallel contract before making the initial *salam* payment

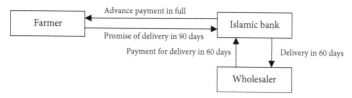

Figure 4.3 *Parallel* salam

to the supplier. The advantage for the wholesaler is that the period until delivery is shorter as the bank will have covered the financing gap. The wholesaler will of course have to pay more than the bank paid initially and the markup on the transaction represents the bank's return for risk taking.[8]

Salam contracts are used today to finance many types of commodity transactions and not only agricultural produce. It is, however, usually a short-term financing facility to cover periods of three or six months. For longer periods there would be too much uncertainty over delivery to use a *salam* contract that involves payment in advance in full. Contracts that involve simultaneous risk sharing between the wholesaler and the bank, such as *musharaka*, may be preferable rather than the sequential risk sharing with *salam* and parallel *salam*.

Salam versus *arboun*

Salam can be considered as a form of forward contract, although the latter do not always involve prepayment of the full amount but rather payment of a deposit to fix the delivery price. With forward contracts and *salam* there is an obligation to pay in full, but not in advance in the case of forwards. Options are different, as with these the financier pays a deposit, but there is no obligation to take delivery. However, if the option is not exercised the client looses their deposit. As options are often used for speculative purposes they are prohibited under *Shari'ah*. The permitted alternative is *arboun*, which also involves a payment in advance, but in this case the payment represents a deposit, the intention of the client being to take delivery and pay the remaining amount. *Arboun* contracts are never traded, whereas options are invariably traded.[9]

Although suppliers receive a guaranteed price with options the asymmetries in the contracts can put them in a disadvantaged position. If the market price is higher than the option price at the time of delivery, the buyer will exercise the option and the suppliers receive less than they would through a spot sale. On the other hand, if the market price is below the price of the option, the holders of the option will not go ahead with the transaction and the supplier will have to sell at the lower spot price. Suppliers are tempted to enter options contracts because of the advance deposits they receive. However, with *arboun* they not only get the deposit money but a guaranteed sale. In other words, *arboun* contracts increase certainty and share risk. In contrast, options contracts increase risk and transfer the risk to the supplier.

Salam is very different from a futures contract which is designed to be traded in an exchange market. With *salam* both the buyer and the seller agree to undertake a transaction in a specified commodity at an agreed time in the future. The transaction will not involve other parties. In contrast, with futures the buyer will sell the contract to another market trader who may be unknown to the seller. There is no personal buyer and seller relationship with a futures contract and no degree of trust. It is the exchange that licences the traders, with those who do not meet their financial commitments expelled. In contrast, with *salam* there is no trading and therefore no exchange costs or margins. In a futures market traders must post a margin or performance bond of at least 5 per cent of the value of the transaction. This covers the counterparty risk the exchange itself runs if payments obligations are not met. As often futures are traded hundreds of times by hundreds of traders before delivery occurs, the market is completely impersonal. Furthermore, most of the transactions are speculative with buyers merely taking long and short positions depending on price expectations rather than actually wanting delivery. Such speculative behaviour, which involves some parties gaining at the expense of others, is completely contrary to Islamic teaching which stresses fairness and justice in transactions. Forward contracts, although they differ from *salam* contracts, are permissible under *Shari'ah* as they are not traded, unlike futures.

Ijara operating leases

With *murabaha* and *salam* contracts the client obtains ownership of the commodities or goods being financed but often businesses and individuals only want to use an asset rather than own it. Leasing provides an obvious solution, the advantage for the client being that they do not have to fund a substantial deposit and, over time, the entire purchase price. In the case of vehicles and equipment, especially IT equipment, clients may not wish to own a rapidly depreciating asset that soon becomes outdated. Through sequential-leasing contracts clients can update the vehicles or equipment they use each time the contract terminates, but also have the assurance that the rent is fixed at the start of each contract period and the payments are agreed and known.[10]

In *ijara* contracts the dates when the rents are payable are usually specified, most being made on a monthly basis.

The amount of the payment may be the same over the entire contract period or fixed with reference to a cost-of-funding index such as the interbank offer rate that prevails in the market. This can be viewed as an interest rate proxy, and therefore arguably *haram*. However, a distinction has to be made between the amount of a payment and the nature of a payment. Under an *ijara* rental contract the payment can be legally designated as rent and not as interest as it is for the usage of the property, the owner of which has speci-fied responsibilities. In contrast, the owner of money has no similar responsibilities as money differs from physical equipment or property which requires maintenance.

In order for *ijara* contracts to be substantive they should take the form of an operating lease rather than a financing lease. The latter resembles a conventional loan agreement as it is a simple financing arrangement which transfers all the risk in maintaining the property or equipment to the lessee. The owner has negligible or even no responsibilities, which raises the question of what justifies the rental and whether it is fair to receive a return for no effort or risk taking. In contrast, with operating leases the owner will be responsible for the external fabric and building's insurance or *takaful* payments in the case of real estate, and mainte-nance costs in the case of equipment or vehicles. The lessee may be responsible for the cleaning and internal furnishing and decoration in the case of a building, and payments for the energy used or repairs due to their negligence in the case of equipment or vehicles. This ensures risks are shared fairly between the parties. The *ijara* contract should be as explicit as possible concerning who is responsible for what.

The structure of an *ijara* operating leasing arrange-ment is illustrated in Figure 4.4. Usually a Special Purpose Vehicle (SPV) is established by the law firm arranging the transaction under instruction from the Islamic investment

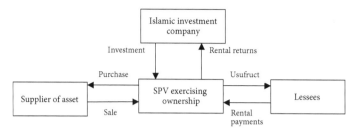

Figure 4.4 Ijara *operating lease*

company which may be an Islamic bank. The company provides sufficient capital so that the SPV can acquire the asset, which may be real estate, equipment or vehicles, through a sale-and-purchase contract.

It is the SPV, a not-for-profit intermediary, that collects the rent from the lessees and pays it to the Islamic investment company. It also exercises ownership rights, and will arrange the sale of the assets the proceeds from which will accrue to the Islamic investment company. Of course, establishing an SPV is not necessarily a prerequisite for an *ijara* contract, but it is convenient for the investors and provides comfort to the lessees. In the case of the Islamic investment company becoming insolvent, there would be no call on the leased assets which would continue to be used by the lessees until the lease expired. The SPV, in other words, ensures the lessees are bankruptcy remote providing the contracts between the investors and the SPV and the lessees and the SPV are appropriately worded. Once the lease expires, however, any revenues from the sale of the asset would accrue to the creditors of the Islamic investment company if it was insolvent and otherwise unable to meet its debt obligations.

Ijara agreements are classified as sale contracts as is the case with *murabaha* but what is being sold is not a commodity as with *murabaha* or *salam* but rather usufruct rights for a specific period, typically three years. At the end of the leasing period the client may have the right to purchase the property or equipment, either at a price which was specified when the contract was signed, or at the market price at the time of the termination of the lease, but in this case the method of valuation should be stated in the contract to avoid uncertainty and possible disputes between the parties. The leased asset may alternatively pass as a gift or *hiba* at the end of the lease period to the lessee, but in this case there will be a higher rent. Where property or equipment passes to the lessee on termination of the contract this represents a hire-purchase agreement, designated *ijara wa iqtina* in the Middle East and *ijara muntahia bi tamleek* in South East Asia. In the latter case the contract contains an option clause for the lessee to purchase the leased asset at the end of the period, but this is at the discretion of the lessee and does not have to be exercised. In contrast, under *ijara wa iqtina* there is a purchase obligation by the lessee.

Istisna'a contracts

Most Islamic financial contracts reviewed so far, apart from *salam* and *arboun*, are for goods or commodities already produced. Whereas *salam* was traditionally used to finance agricultural production over the harvesting cycle, *istisna'a* was used for manufacturing production. Often manufacturing takes a considerable amount of time, years rather than months, and hence whereas *salam* and *arboun* contracts typically run for three to six months, *istisna'a* can cover periods of three to five years or even longer. Today it is the preferred contract for project financing largely because of its versatility and inherent characteristics.[11] Given the large number of projects requiring finance in the GCC (Gulf Cooperation Council) and South East Asia as a result of development spending both by governments and private

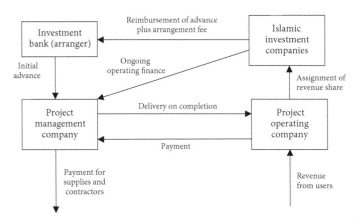

Figure 4.5 Istisna'a *project finance*

companies, *istisna'a* is becoming increasingly significant, with some financing for amounts exceeding $1 billion.

Istisna'a structures are usually complex given the many parties involved, the large amounts of finance required and the risks for each of the parties. A typical structure is illustrated in Figure 4.5 with an investment bank acting as arranger and providing the initial advance to the project management company to cover payments to contractors and sub-contractors as well as, in some cases, payment for supplies including raw materials. On completion the project is handed over to an operating company which collects the revenue from the users as illustrated.

The investment bank could continue funding the project and eventually benefit from the revenue from the users but this is unlikely as most investment banks do not want to have their funds tied up and illiquid for periods of many years. Rather their competency is in project appraisal and the arrangement of finance. Investment banks are driven by fees from their clients, not by a desire to obtain returns from their own long-term investments. Therefore, they are more likely to bring in Islamic investment companies, which include *Shari'ah*-compliant asset managers, through a parallel transaction as shown in Figure 4.5. These companies could of course invest directly in the project rather than have an investment bank involved, but they may lack project appraisal skills and the necessary resources to individually provide the initial advances. Hence the parallel transaction involves splitting, with for example the investment bank providing an initial advance of $1 billion, but ten Islamic investment companies each contributing $100 million to the reimbursement, plus a share of whatever fee is payable to the investment bank for its work.

Once the investment bank exits it may move on to new *istisna'a* arrangements, with the Islamic investment companies who are now involved with the project for the long term left as the sole beneficiaries of the share of the user revenue which accrues to the financiers. Their benefits may accrue for a period of ten years or more, whatever is stipulated in the initial agreement negotiated by the investment bank, the project management company and the project operating company. The proceeds may be directly related to the user fees, or alternatively through a series of fixed or variable payments which are deducted from the revenue. The former may be regarded as more legitimate from an Islamic perspective as it involves a greater degree of risk sharing, but if the fixed or variable payments are contingent on specified target revenues this also involves risk sharing, albeit to a more limited degree.

There are considerable risks associated with long-term project finance not least that the project management company could become insolvent and unable to continue its work. Usually project finance involves complementary contracts such as bid bonds from companies tendering for the contract which are bank guarantees that the management company is creditworthy. A clause may be written into the Islamic financing contract specifying that bid bonds are required. Performance bonds are often required by the operating company to provide compensation if the project is not completed on time or as specified. The management company will have to arrange and cover the costs of such bonds. Again a requirement for performance bonds may be written into the Islamic financing contract. It should be noted that although such guarantees are designated as bonds, there are no interest charges, rather fees and compensation payments.

Participatory financing contracts

Mudaraba and *musharaka* contracts were much favoured by Islamic scholars because of their inherent risk-sharing characteristics. They can be classified as providing equity-participatory finance rather than debt finance, although the status of the financiers differs from that of those investing in company equity through stock markets or private equity placements who are subject to greater risks. Both *mudaraba* and *musharaka* involve partnership contracts, but in the former only the *rabb al maal*, the financier, provides capital, with the *mudarib* providing management skills and effort. In contrast, with *musharaka* all the partners subscribe to the capital required by the business.[12]

Both contracts provide for profit sharing, usually in proportion to the investments made, although there can be flexibility over the proportionate shares as long as this is agreed by all the partners. Loss sharing is strictly proportionate to the capital contributions. This is regarded as just as the capital contributions are indicative of the partner's ability to absorb losses with those who invest the most entitled to the greatest profit share, but also taking on the largest exposure to any losses. As in *mudaraba* contracts the *mudarib* makes no financial contribution, they have no liability for losses. As the *mudarib* shares in profits, however, in the event of losses there will be nothing to share and they will receive no remuneration.

Although, as discussed in Chapter 3, *mudaraba* contracts are used for investment deposits in Islamic banks they are little used for financing, except in the case of restricted *mudaraba* where the funding comes entirely from the depositors with the banks role confined to recipient appraisal and the administration of payments. *Musharaka* is used to a greater extent but only where the contract is modified, where it takes on the characteristics of a debt agreement rather than being an equity placement. Islamic banks, like their conventional equivalents, have expertise in the appraisal and management of credit risk, but deposit-taking banks have to limit their direct exposure to market risk, not least because of regulatory requirements, an issue dealt with in Chapter 7.

The main purpose of *musharaka* contracts is to protect the partners from each other's actions. Usually those participating in a joint-venture scheme are in accord at the start otherwise they would not sign the contracts. Unfortunately, all too often if the scheme starts to perform badly or makes losses, individual investors may opt to pull out, even if this adversely affects the material interests of their fellow investors. *Musharaka* contracts prevent this happening by tying the investors into the agreement for a predetermined period of time unless there are exceptional circumstances, such as the death or life-threatening illness of a particular investor, circumstances that must be spelt out in detail in the clauses of the contract.

The differences between *musharaka* and equity investment are illustrated in Table 4.4. Equity contracts and

Table 4.4 Musharaka *versus equity investment contracts*

Musharaka	Equity investment
Venture of limited duration	Company exists in perpetuity
Partnership with joint ownership	Individual shareholdings
No exit without agreement of partners	Exit at any time if company listed
Investors obtain profit share	Investors paid dividends
Less concern with asset values on termination	Focus on capital gains and market value of the equity

the concept of limited-liability companies owe nothing to religious teaching whereas *musharaka* is a contract which pre-dated Islam but was refined in traditional *fiqh mua-malat* to ensure there was justice to all the parties. In other words, *musharaka* contracts can be classified as *Shari'ah* based whereas equity contracts are at best *Shari'ah* compliant, assuming that the portfolio of investments are *halal*, an issue that will be explored further in Chapter 10 when examining fund management.

Musharaka partnerships are typically established to last for three to five years. In contrast a company exists in perpetuity unless it is taken over or merged with another company or becomes bankrupt. As indicated in Table 4.4, *musharaka* contracts are a partnership arrangement with collective rather than individual rights and obligations, but shareholders in a company are primarily concerned with their own interests if these diverge from those of the company. If the company is listed on a stock market investors are free to sell their shares at any time without consulting the other shareholders or even knowing the identity of the buyers. Where the company is not listed and the investments are in the form of private equity placements there may, however, be restrictions on exit. Finally, with most equity investments investors are aiming to make capital gains rather than receiving dividends; indeed, in the past many preferred to see income reinvested rather than paid out to shareholders, although attitudes to income have changed as a result of the global financial crisis of 2008 with more stress on dividends than before. In contrast, with *musharaka* there is less discretion to reduce profit payouts as these are the incentives for the investors rather than the prospect of capital gains. In some *musharaka* agreements investors receive their invested capital back in nominal terms when the contract expires, although in such cases the contracts become debt instruments, but of course the returns are not predetermined, only the capital repayment.

Notes

1. Sami Tamer, *The Islamic Financial System* (Frankfurt: Peter Lang European University Studies, 2005), pp. 78–80.
2. Ibrahim A. Mardam-Bey, 'Recent developments in Islamic auto finance products', in Sohail Jaffer (ed.), *Islamic Retail Banking and Finance: Global Challenges and Opportunities* (London: Euromoney Books, 2005), pp. 107–12.
3. Rodney Wilson, *The Development of Islamic Finance in the GCC*, Kuwait Programme on Development, Governance and Globalisation in the Gulf States (London: London School of Economics, 2009), p. 20.
4. http://www.kfh.com/en/commercial/cars/new-cars.aspx.
5. http://www.alrajhibank.com.sa/en/personal/home-finance/pages/buy-home.aspx.
6. Mohammad Nejatullah Siddiqi, 'Economics of *tawarruq*: how its *mafasid* overwhelm the *masalih*', paper presented to the Harvard Islamic Finance Workshop, Harvard Law School, 2007.
7. *Fiqh* Academy, May 2009, Sharjah, Resolution 179 (19/5).

8. Zamir Iqbal, 'Financial engineering in Islamic finance', *Thunderbird International Business Review*, 41: 4–5, July–October 1999, p. 541–59.

9. Humayon Dar, 'Incentive compatibility of Islamic financing', in Kabir Hassan and Mervyn Lewis (eds), *Handbook of Islamic Banking* (Cheltenham: Edward Elgar, 2007), pp. 85–95.

10. Zamir Iqbal and Abbas Mirakhor, *An Introduction to Islamic Finance: Theory and Practice*, 2nd edn (Singapore: Wiley Finance, 2011), pp. 80–2.

11. Muhammad Anas Zarqa, '*Istisna'a* financing of infrastructure projects', *Islamic Economic Studies*, 4: 2, May 1997, pp. 67–74.

12. Malcolm Harper, '*Musharaka* partnership financing: an approach to venture capital for microenterprise', *Small Enterprise Development*, 5: 4, December 1994, pp. 27–36.

CHAPTER 5

LAWS PROVIDING FOR COMPREHENSIVE ISLAMIC BANKING SYSTEMS

In most jurisdictions Islamic banks coexist with conventional banks, both of whom compete for clients. Despite the growth of Islamic banks they usually only account for a limited share of total bank deposits or total bank assets, often less than 10 per cent of the total. Although the percentage is rising, there is no market in which conventional banks operate where an Islamic bank is the market leader. There are some countries where the largest conventional banks provide Islamic financial products as is the case with the National Commercial Bank in Saudi Arabia or Maybank in Malaysia, but although this may boost the share of Islamic banks, such provision is often a defensive strategy to prevent Islamic banks achieving market dominance.

An obvious consequence of Islamic banks having a minority share of the market is that they tend to follow existing banking models and processes, or in other words to be market followers rather than market leaders. In some cases conventional financing contracts are taken as the template and modified in minor ways to ensure *Shariʻah*-board approval. All too often the returns to depositors and financing charges correspond to those offered by conventional banks as the Islamic banks are price takers rather than price makers. There may be qualitative differences in the products offered but in a competitive market pricing tends to be similar, or indeed less advantageous, for Islamic bank clients given *Shari'ah* compliance costs.

Politics, ideology and Islamic finance

One way of overcoming the inevitable limitations and short-comings of Islamic banking in a so-called dual system is to enact legislation converting the entire system to being based on *Shari'ah* principles. This has the advantage of eliminating the difficulties of offering Islamic financial services in a market dominated by conventional banks. However, it also eliminates choice and is potentially detrimental for competition. In such a situation there may be less incentive to innovate and employee motivation may also be an issue if they are unenthusiastic about Islamic finance but that is their only option because of the law.

Only two countries, Iran and the Sudan, have enacted legislation converting their banking systems to being fully Islamic, although in the case of Pakistan a blueprint for an Islamic banking system was commissioned but this was never enacted.[1] In the case of Sudan, the original law of 1984 which provided for all banking to be *Shari'ah* compliant was superseded by a law in 1993 establishing a *Shari'ah* Supervisory Council within the Central Bank to oversee the system. This was in turn superseded by the Business Banking Act of 2003 which was designed to provide greater regulatory clarity. Chapter III of this Act provides for a Higher Shariah Control Commission which took over the duties of the former Supervisory Council. The Act of 2003 spells out how the Control Commission was to be established, the remuneration conditions for its president and its objectives, functions and powers.

After obtaining recognition as a separate state, South Sudan enacted its own law in July 2011. A new Central Bank has been established for South Sudan which is largely non-Muslim. The *Shari'ah* Supervisory Council has no formal authority with respect to South Sudan which no longer has any Islamic banks.

Iran's Islamic banking system

As Iran is the only country which has converted to and sustained an Islamic financial system it is pertinent to examine its experience to see what lessons can be derived. Iran's Law on Usury- (Interest-) Free Banking of 1983 was enacted four years after the Islamic Republic was declared and must be viewed in the context of the politics of that time. Article 1 of the law provides for the establishment of a monetary and credit system based on rightness and justice as delineated by Islamic jurisprudence. The implication is that this will be free of *riba*, which the current English translation of Iran's Banking Law equates with both usury and interest, although this was ambiguous in earlier translations which only specified usury.

The main support for introducing an Islamic financial system into Iran came from Abdulhassan Banisadr, the first president of the Islamic Republic, who wrote a doctoral thesis on Islamic banking for the Sorbonne in Paris. Banisadr's presidency lasted only just over one year however, as he soon fell out with Ayatollah Khomeini, and as a result he was impeached in June 1981, two years before the Islamic banking law was finally enacted. Despite widespread support in the *majlis*, the Iranian parliament, there was confusion about how an Islamic banking system would actually operate. It was largely through the efforts of Bank Markazi (Iran's Central Bank) that the new law was drafted, but the staff of the commercial banks were sceptical and unenthusiastic, and although these institutions were state owned, they enjoyed considerable autonomy. It was only in 1985 that *Shari'ah*-compliant financing was introduced, and most deposits were not Islamised until 1987.

Iran's Islamic banking law provides for deposits on a *qard hasan* basis, the concept being that of an interest-free loan by depositors to the bank, the only type of lending permitted under *Shari'ah*. However, those who drafted the law recognised that depositors expect some return, especially in inflationary conditions. Hence, Article 6 of the law provides for non-fixed bonuses in cash or in kind. In practice prizes are given to depositors, with the lucky account holders selected through a lottery.[2] As gambling (*maisir*) is forbidden in Quranic teaching (*Sura* 2: 219) it is unclear how awarding such prizes can be viewed as justified, especially as most depositors, as in any lottery, do not receive prizes.

Article 3 of Iran's Islamic banking law provides for term-investment deposits which the banks can use for *mudaraba* financing and direct investments, the so-called restricted *mudaraba* which the influential Iraqi Shia cleric, Muhammad Baqir As Sadr, recommended.[3] With restricted *mudaraba* contracts the bank acts as an agent and the depositor shares in the profits from the project being financed rather than receiving interest. The contract is regarded as just, as the depositor as financier (*rabb al maal*) is sharing in the risk with the businessmen or entrepreneur (*mudarib*) undertaking the project. In practice, term-investment deposit rates in Iran are determined by the Bank Markazi at the macroeconomic level and are unrelated to the performance or profitability at the microeconomic level of particular projects. For 2009, for example, the term deposit rates for one year were 14.5 per cent rising to 17.5 per cent for five-year deposits,[4] these rates largely reflecting inflationary expectations, a subject on which *fiqh* is silent.

State-directed banking in Iran

In contrast to the customer-driven Islamic banking in the GCC, on the Iranian side of the Gulf the policies have been dictated by the government's economic priorities. Under Article 10 of Iran's Fourth Five-Year Development Plan, covering the period from 2005 to 2010, the allocation of banking facilities by sector and region was undertaken through cash subsidies which were approved at Cabinet level.[5] One quarter of bank credit was to be allocated to agriculture under the Fourth Plan, 35 per cent to manufacturing and mining, 20 per cent to construction and housing and 8 per cent to exports. As almost half of Iran's GDP is accounted for by services and only 10 per cent by agriculture, 11 per cent by industry and mining and 5 per cent by construction, the financing allocations in the Fourth Plan were clearly distorted.

Article 11 of the section of the Fourth Plan dealing with credit policy states that the banks are obliged to give priority in their lending to deprived and less-developed regions and technologically advanced projects. While the former may be commendable from a social perspective, the article is contradictory, as high-technology projects are unlikely to be located in such areas. Under Article 12 housing finance is solely for construction and not for mortgages on existing properties. This is unhelpful for the development of a housing market in Iran, and limits the return that investors can expect from housing or commercial property.

Such quotas and restrictions mean that potentially profitable projects may not get undertaken while resources are channelled to sectors and areas where returns may be low. The quotas have resulted in an inefficient allocation of capital, with banks autonomy to make financing decisions based on normal risk and return criteria severely curtailed. However, under Article 23 the Central Bank Guidelines encourage credit scoring, with banks urged to favour customers with good credit records and limiting credit to those who have not met their debt obligations by at least the amount of the outstanding debt.

Although the allocation of finance by the banks in Iran is state directed at the sector level, the economy is gradually coming under private rather than state control. The propor-tion of commercial bank assets accounted for by claims on the non-public sector increased from 47 per cent in 2004–5 to over 54.5 per cent by 2008–9.[6] Over the same period the amount allocated to public corporations declined from 5 per cent to a mere 1.3 per cent. Deposits with the Central Bank increased from 7.7 per cent to almost 10 per cent, but this was largely because banks were required to hold more liquidity against contingencies due to the uncertain economic climate.

Liberalisation of banking in Iran and the role of private banks

The public-sector banks in Iran appear to be becoming more autonomous in their decision making, a development welcomed by the Central Bank which appears to recognise that there are efficiency gains from liberalisation. In particular, the use of commercial criteria rather than politi-cal patronage is implicitly supported, although the term political patronage is not of course used in Central Bank publications. Nevertheless it is asserted that credit poli-cies can affect sector growth rates. There was a reduction in direct controls over credit which meant the 'free' allocation increased from 35 per cent in 2004 to 75 per cent in 2008.[7] Although there has been no plan to privatise Iran's major commercial banks, which have been under state owner- ship since 1979, there is no ideological objection to private banking by the authorities in Iran. The nationalisation was simply driven by expediency, as without state support in the aftermath of the revolution the banks would have become bankrupt. There was enormous capital flight in the late 1970s with a substantial run down in bank deposits as upper- and middle-class Iranians, especially those influential under the Shah, left the country for a life in exile. Arguably the inef- ficiencies in the allocation of finance and the poor resultant returns was a result of government directives which would have applied regardless of whether the banks were under public or private ownership.

Giving the state-run commercial banks more autonomy is a necessary, though not sufficient, condition to improve their performance. One issue is the banking culture, which can be categorised in Iran as relationship banking, with long-term continuity in the relationships between the banks and their clients. Relationship banking has the virtue of reducing contracting and monitoring costs, but the down- side is that it can also result in cronyism and even corrup- tion. Merely because the banks are in theory Islamic and are supposed to uphold Muslim religious values will not ensure that all employees behave honestly and responsibly, espe- cially when effective enforcement mechanisms to reduce operational risk are absent. Bank Markazi, like other central banks, has a supervision department whose remit includes the prevention of financial crime, but its major concern is 'about the fitness and propriety of the staff nominated by the banks for taking up posts of a managerial nature (assist- ant manager and above) in the banks' overseas branches'[8] and not the local staff. The worry is about the finance of illegal imports, evasion of taxes and money laundering by clients, and not the relationship of bank managers and clients.

In 2001, in response to lobbying by industry, there was a significant policy change in Iran permitting the establishment of private banks. Bank Eghtesad Novin (EN Bank) was the first institution established, which is owned by a group of construction and industrial companies including Behshahr, Behpak and Novin, with Bank Melli, the largest state-owned bank, together with the civil servants' pension fund, having a minority stake. Given this ownership it is clear that the dividing line between state and private ownership is blurred in Iran. More important than the actual ownership was the ethos of EN Bank, the aim being to provide more modern and innovative banking services for bank clients in line with international standards, rather than having the bureaucratic form-filling approach of the state-owned commercial banks. EN Bank obtained a stock-market listing in 2004 and by 2008 its assets exceeded $9.4 billion.

Parsian Bank, which was also established in 2001, has experienced even more rapid growth with its total assets worth almost $22 billion by 2010, making it the largest of the six private banks in Iran. This compares with the total assets of just under $60 billion of Bank Melli, illustrating the increasing significance of the private banks, which now account for over 16 per cent of total financing.[9] As on the Arab side of the Gulf, the private banks are focused on consumer finance, especially vehicle and housing funding. This contrasts with the state-owned commercial banks that are mainly involved in corporate finance, particularly import finance. The private banks are aiming to gain personal customers by offering an attractive range of accounts, and encourage those with salaries to arrange direct transfers to their current accounts. In marketing terms the focus is on middle-class and more affluent customers. The majority of Iranians, and virtually all of the poorer classes, do not use banks, most household payments being in cash.

The Islamic credentials of Iran's banking system

In traditional Islamic societies markets, including credit markets, were overseen by the *hisba*, a moral enforcement agency to ensure fairness and justice, usually controlled by the state. Religious guidance was provided by the *muhtasib*, a scholar versed in *fiqh*. There was no attempt to establish such an institutional framework in Iran, either during the Islamic revolution or subsequently. The Central Bank of Iran conducts monetary and supervisory policy in the same manner as any other equivalent body internationally, although the terminology used conforms to that of Islamic finance. There is a stress on form, but in reality there is little substantial difference with conventional monetary policy.

The Monetary and Credit Council of Iran's Central Bank determines the profit rates paid for commercial bank financing, raising the rate to control inflation or reducing it to stimulate the demand for finance. As inflation has been a continuing problem in Iran, with the rate in 2009 peaking at 20.9 per cent, monetary tightening has been the norm, partly to counteract the stimulus effects from high levels of government current spending, especially on subsidies. The other major instruments of monetary policy in Iran include credit ceilings, reserve requirements ratios, open-market operations involving so-called participation papers and open-deposit accounts with the Central Bank. These operate in much the same way as on the Arab side of the Gulf, the only difference being that instead of referring to interest rates, the participation papers and the open deposits pay profit rates, but as a Central Bank is a financial regulator, not a business focused on profit, it is unclear what the profit rates actually represent.

Table 5.1 shows the types of Islamic financing provided by the different categories of banks in Iran. Farsi terms are used, *gharz-al-hasaneh* being what is transliterated in Arabic as *qard hasan*, an interest-free loan. Banks can levy an arrangement fee and a management charge to cover the administrative costs of such loans, but they must not earn a surplus, as this would represent *riba*. Not surprisingly little *gharz-al-hasaneh* is provided by the private banks in Iran. *Mozarebeh* (*mudaraba* in Arabic) is more widely offered by the private banks, a contract whereby the bank advances funds to a business in return for a share in its profits. Partnership contracts (*musharaka* in Arabic) are even more popular, whereby the bank and the business both invest in a new venture and share the profits according to a predeter-mined ratio. Commercial banks use forward transactions (*salam*) for financing, this referring to a contract whereby the financier pays in full in advance for a commodity, usu-ally agricultural output, to be supplied at a future date. The advances can be used by farmers to cover the costs of seeds and fertilizers, as well as paying their workers. *Joaleh* (*wakala* in Arabic) is where an amount of money is advanced to an agent for a specific investment. The agent is paid a manage-ment fee but the investment and any returns remain the property of the bank. Of greater significance are instalment sales (*ijara wa iqtina* in Arabic) whereby the bank purchases equipment or vehicles on behalf of a client, with the client then paying rent for its use and making repayments over a three-year period after which ownership will be transferred to the client. This is the most important method of financ-ing by the state-owned banks in Iran, especially by special-ised institutions such as the Bank of Industry and Mining,

Table 5.1 *Islamic financing facilities in Iran (%)*

	Commercial banks	Specialised banks	Private banks
Gharz-al-hasaneh	4.8	2.3	0.7
Mozarebeh	4.9	0.6	18.0
Forward transactions	4.4	2.0	0.0
Partnerships	13.8	11.7	42.1
Joaleh	6.0	1.2	2.2
Installment sale	47.2	71.8	11.2
Direct investment	0.9	0.1	1.0
Other	18.0	10.3	24.8

Source: Central Bank of Iran (2010).

Bank Keshavarzi and Bank Maskan. For the private banks partnership financing appears to be more significant, possibly because the expected returns are higher reflecting the risks involved.

The effect of sanctions on Iran's Islamic banking system

The United States has maintained sanctions on Iran since the American embassy hostage crisis in 1979 following the Islamic revolution. Initially the sanctions were on Iranian-US trade, but they were widened because of Iran's nuclear programme involving uranium enrichment. In 2007, sanctions were applied to Bank Melli and Bank Saderat, and these were extended to Bank Mellat in 2009. As Bank Melli is the largest Islamic bank in the world the question arises as to how far sanctions have damaged the Islamic banking industry, primarily in Iran, but also elsewhere where the banks subject to sanctions have a significant presence.

So far the sanctions have had little impact on Iran's overseas bank branches. The current resolution on sanctions agreed with the Europeans and Russia through the United Nations Security Council 'calls upon states to take appropriate measures that prohibit the opening of new Iranian bank branches or offices abroad if there is reason to suspect they might be aiding Iran's nuclear or missile programs'.[10] It also calls on states 'to exercise vigilance over transactions involving Iranian banks, including the Central Bank of Iran, to ensure that those transactions do not aid Tehran's nuclear and missile programs'. It is unlikely that this will affect the activities of Bank Melli or other Iranian banks in Europe or the GCC, not least because any financial connections with enriching uranium or missile development will be difficult to prove.

Partly as a result of pressure from the United States, the European Union has further tightened its sanctions on Iran from August 2010, with prior authorisation required for transfers of funds exceeding €40,000, and Japan introduced restrictions on dealing with fifteen Iranian banks. Russia, although a member of the quartet that aims at peaceful conflict resolution in the Middle East, has not imposed sanctions, nor has China, Iran's major trading partner.

Although it is too early to determine the impact of EU and Japanese sanctions, the impact of US sanctions on the banking system appears to be minimal. Bank deposits increased by almost 79 per cent over the period from 2006 to 2010, and financing for the private sector increased even faster. Admittedly some of the increase reflected inflation, which has been high in Iran, peaking at 20.9 per cent in 2009 as already mentioned, but it has subsequently fallen back to 7.4 per cent.

The recent financial performance of Parsian Bank, Iran's largest private bank, shown in Table 5.2, exhibits a strong upward trend in deposits and financing. As the figures are in US dollars, distortions due to inflation are less of

Table 5.2 *The financial performance of Parsian Bank (in $ million)*

	2008	2009	2010
Total assets	16,382	19,548	21,915
Financing	11,416	13,847	15,183
Deposits	14,452	17,324	19,564
Total income	2,353	2,989	3,612
Depositor income	1,751	2,275	2,655
Net profit	332	338	399

Source: Parsian Bank, *Annual Report* (Tehran, 2010), p. 16.

an issue. Depositors enjoyed significant income distributions, yet there was still reasonable profits recorded which benefited shareholders. Admittedly Parsian Bank has the highest return on assets of any Iranian bank, 2.13 per cent, below the 4.03 per cent return of Riyadh-based Al Rajhi Bank for the same period, but higher than Kuwait Finance House's 0.27 per cent.[11] The latter was adversely affected by the global financial crisis, but this had much less impact on Iran's relatively isolated economy, partly closed because of sanctions. In other words, sanctions may actually have proved beneficial. The links between Iran and China's rapidly growing economy have been more advantageous than any links there might have been with the sluggish United States economy had sanctions been relaxed.

Conclusions from Iran's experience

Enacting ambitious Islamic banking legislation to transform a country's entire financial system may have less impact than those who had been ideologically inspired to achieve this goal had hoped. There has been a degree of drift in Iran's banking system and there are few outside advocates of Islamic finance who look to the Islamic Republic's banking system as a model to follow. Indeed operationally it is more similar to conventional systems than the legislation suggests and indeed not so different to what preceded it before the revolution. The same banks and their staff remained in place. For more innovative and interesting models of Islamic banking it is arguably more relevant to look to dual banking systems, the subject of the next chapter.

Notes

1. International Institute of Islamic Economics, *Blueprint of Islamic Financial System*, Islamabad, 1999.
2. Bank Melli, *Annual Report* (Tehran, 2007), p. 11.
3. Rodney Wilson, 'The contribution of Muhammad Baqir Al-Sadr to contemporary Islamic economic thought', *Journal of Islamic Studies*, 9: 1, 1998, pp. 46–59.
4. Central Bank of Islamic Republic of Iran, 2009–10, p. 16.
5. Central Bank of Iran, *Supervisory Policy Guidelines.*
6. Central Bank of Iran, *Annual Review*, 2008–9, p. 72.
7. Central Bank of Iran, *Economic Report*, 2008, p. 101.
8. Central Bank of Iran, *Bank Supervision Department*, 2010.
9. Central Bank of Iran, *Economic Report*, 2008, p. 72.
10. *Reuters*, 2010.

CHAPTER 6
LAWS PROVIDING FOR PARALLEL ISLAMIC BANKING SYSTEMS

In most jurisdictions where Islamic banks operate, apart from Iran, they have to compete with conventional banks involved in interest-based borrowing and lending. The legal framework governing the licensing of banks and their regulation was designed primarily for conventional institutions, not least as there were no Islamic banks in existence in most cases when the banking laws were drafted. Three choices therefore arise: firstly, whether Islamic banks can be accommodated within existing legal provision, whether the existing banking legislation requires amendment or, more radically, whether new legislation is necessary.

In the latter case special, or more controversially discriminatory, treatment may be deemed to be necessary. If this is the case then the question arises about what is the objective or purpose of the legislation? Is it to favour Islamic banking and encourage its development, which may be at the expense of the conventional banks, or is it simply to create a level playing field where Islamic and conventional banks can compete on the same footing? There is also the issue of whether Islamic banking legislation is merely a political statement of support, or if it has substance reflecting the particular needs of Islamic banks and the constraints they are morally bound to work under in the interests of *Shari'ah* compliance.

To highlight the choices and dilemmas specific examples are used for illustrative purposes in this chapter. In particular the Islamic Banking Act of 1983 in Malaysia is examined in detail as well as the United Arab Emirates Federal Law Number 6 of 1985 covering Islamic banks, financial institutions and investment companies. The substantial revisions in 2003 to the Banking Laws of Kuwait are also examined. The legislative changes in the United Kingdom introduced in separate Finance Acts as part of the annual budgetary processes are considered, these mainly affecting the tax treatment of Islamic financing contracts. The United Kingdom experience, as a largely non-Muslim country, is of particular interest as it sets a precedent for the Western world more generally.

Elsewhere much of the provision for Islamic banking is at the regulatory level, and will therefore be dealt with in Chapter 7. This includes the recent regulations in Indonesia issued in 2009 providing for the conversion of commercial banking activity to being *Shari'ah* compliant as well as the coverage of Islamic finance in the rulebooks of Bahrain and Qatar.

The Islamic Banking Act of 1983 in Malaysia

The advocacy of Islamic finance in Malaysia has to be viewed in a political context as it was supported by the United Malay National Organisation (UMNO), the party which has dominated politics since independence. Tabung Haji, a savings bank which Bumiputera Muslims used to accumulate the funds necessary for Hajj travel and expenses, was extremely popular because of its Islamic credentials, especially amongst UMNO supporters. Therefore, when it was proposed to launch an Islamic bank in 1983 which would attempt to apply the lessons from Tabung Haji to commercial finance, the government wanted to play a supportive role. Hence an Islamic Banking Act was passed, more as a gesture of political support rather than because of the need to provide a distinctive legal framework.[1]

Unlike the Law on Interest-Free Banking in Iran discussed in the last chapter, which refers to and attempts to define specific Islamic financing methods, the Malaysian Act makes no such attempt. The Act was pioneering in the sense that it was the first to provide for the regulation of Islamic banking in a common-law jurisdiction, but its distinctive features were limited. The licensing and financial requirements were virtually identical to those of conventional banks in Malaysia, as were the ownership and management provisions and the restrictions on business. From a regulatory perspective nothing seemed to be different. In short, despite the designation of the Banking Act as 'Islamic', there was relatively little content that could be described as *Shari'ah* based or *Shari'ah* compliant.

In Part II of the Act that deals with licensing, Section 5 states that permission to operate will not be given if the aims and operations of the banking business involve any element not approved by the 'Religion of Islam'. Just what these 'elements' might be is not specified, not least as the Malaysian government and Parliament are secular in nature despite the references to Islam in the constitution. Therefore, in legislation it would be inappropriate to indicate what should be approved or not approved in the name of Islam.[2]

In Section 5 the Act states that in the articles of association of the Islamic bank there should be provision for the establishment of a *Shari'ah* advisory board to advise on the operations of the bank and ensure they are not contrary to Islamic teaching. In other words, within each bank there is discretion by the *Shari'ah* board to indicate what is permissible and what is not. There is no indication of what the size of the *Shariʻah* board should be, how its membership should be chosen, or to whom they should be accountable. These provisions were introduced long before the Central Bank of Malaysia established its own *Shariʻah* board and the appointment of *Shariʻah* board members of individual banks was centralised. Section 11 of the Act provides for the revocation of an Islamic bank's licence if it is engaged in any business not approved of by the Religion of Islam. The Act is silent, however, concerning who should make this judgement. It is improbable that those serving on a bank's *Shariʻah* board would recommend the revocation of its licence as then they would be out of a job. It is only since the Islamic Financial Service Board was established that such potential conflicts of interest were identified, but their resolution has yet to be put on a statutory basis.

The other provision of the Act which has been changed is the restriction on foreign-owned banks providing Islamic banking services under Article 6. This was relaxed to allow Al Rajhi Bank of Saudi Arabia and Kuwait Finance House to enter the Malaysian market as part of the drive during the last decade to make Kuala Lumpur an international Islamic financial centre. Under Part III of the Act Islamic banks are obliged to hold reserve funds including liquid deposits at the Central Bank and Government Investment Certificates, provision which is the same as that for conventional banks. This requirement is problematic for Islamic banks as they cannot accept the interest from liquid deposits or the returns from Government Investment Certificates, which are also in the form of interest payments. Islamic monetary instruments have been introduced in recent years in Malaysia but there have been no amendments to the Islamic bank legislation to reflect these developments.

Part V of the Act covers restrictions on business but these are not specific to Islamic banking and merely follow the restrictions applied to conventional banks. The clauses under this heading refer to lending and borrower relations, but Islamic banks cannot provide loans except under *qard hasan* where no interest is charged. There is no reference to this in the legislation.

In short, although the Islamic Banking Act of 1983 was a commendable attempt to ensure that Islamic bank operations in Malaysia were put on a sound footing and there is comprehensive coverage of banking issues, there is little reference to the unique features of Islamic banking or provision for the specific requirements of *Shari'ah*-based financing. There has been much progress on these matters over the last three decades in Malaysia, but this has not yet been reflected in the legislation which remains largely unchanged.

United Arab Emirates Federal Law 6 of 1985

The first commercial Islamic financial institution in the world, Dubai Islamic Bank, started business in 1975 in a legal vacuum as there was no banking law of any kind until the Union Banking Law of 1980, which was the first attempt to legislate for banking at federal level and establish a Central Bank. Hitherto the banks in each emirate had been regulated, largely informally, by the emirates in which they were based, but there was no consistency which created challenges for banks seeking to establish offices in other emirates. Initially this was not an issue for Dubai Islamic Bank whose branches were confined to its home emirate, but as the economy of the UAE became more integrated, the bank opened branches elsewhere, starting with Abu Dhabi.

The aim of Federal Law 6 was not to replace the earlier Union Banking Law which governed conventional as well as Islamic banks but rather to make additional provision for

Islamic banks to supplement the existing law. The new law covered not only Islamic banks but other institutions which were designated as Islamic including investment companies. This meant the UAE Central Bank had a more comprehensive remit that included the entire financial sector and not solely banking activity.[3]

Under Article 3 of the Law Islamic banks have the right to establish new companies and participate in existing companies provided the companies are managed in conformity with *Shari'ah*. This is a wide remit which goes beyond the usual constraints of deposit-taking institutions that do not normally undertake direct investment because of perceived market risk. Critics could argue that *Shari'ah* compliance provides cover for more risky operations which could potentially increase systemic risk for the entire financial system, but there is no evidence that this has occurred in practice and that the behaviour of Islamic financial institutions has been more reckless than that of their conventional counterparts. On the contrary, those in the UAE seem to be cautious and conservative risk managers.

Islamic investment companies have the right under Article 3.2 to undertake all kinds of financial services, including not only investment in movable assets, but also deposit taking. This arguably blurs the distinction between banks and investment companies and raises the issue of whether the UAE Central Bank would be obliged to safeguard the funds of investors which are classified as deposits and whether deposit guarantees apply. Normally those placing funds in investment companies do not have such guarantees.

Under Article 4 of Federal Law 6 Islamic banks and investment companies are exempted from the provisions of Clause (a) of Article 90 of the Union Banking Law. This is very significant as the latter prohibits commercial banks from carrying out, on their own account, commercial or industrial activities or acquiring or owning traded goods except in the settlement of debts. The purpose of this exemption is to enable Islamic banks in the UAE to undertake *murabaha* transactions which involve the bank directly purchasing and reselling commodities. Exemption is also given to Clause (b) of Article 90 which prohibits banks from owning immovable property apart from that used for their own premises. The exemption enables Islamic banks in the UAE to undertake *ijara* with respect to real-estate leasing which involves the direct ownership of immovable assets. There is also ownership involved with *musharaka* and diminishing *musharaka* which can also be accommodated under this exemption.

Islamic banks and investment companies are also exempt from Clause (e) of Article 96 of the Union Law of 1980 which provides for interest to be paid on bank deposits and the collection of interest and commission from customers. This exemption is to ensure that Islamic banks and investment companies in the UAE do not become involved with the payment or receipt of interest which is equated with the *riba* prohibited in *Shari'ah*.

The UAE Federal Law 6 was the first law anywhere to deal explicitly with *Shari'ah* supervisory issues. Article 5 provides for the establishment of a Higher *Shari'ah* Authority subject to cabinet approval comprising of legal and banking personnel. The Authority was to have responsibility to ensure that Islamic banks and investment companies operating within the UAE were compliant with *Shari'ah* law. The Authority was also empowered to offer its opinions on *Shari'ah* financial matters to agencies in the UAE, presumably including the Central Bank, although this is not specified. Article 5 does, however, specify that the rulings of the Higher *Shari'ah* Authority would be binding on the agencies seeking its advice.

In the event, despite the legal provision, the Higher *Shari'ah* Authority was never appointed. It might have been more effective to have given the UAE Central Bank the responsibility for establishing the Authority and appointing its members, as in the Malaysian case, rather than referring this to the Federal Cabinet who have so many issues to deal with and have less financial expertise. It is perhaps unfortunate that Article 5 stipulates that the Authority should be attached to the Ministry of Justice and Islamic Affairs. Nevertheless the provision for an Authority remains and activating this statutory power remains an option without the need for any further legislation apart from perhaps a technical amendment to Article 5.

Article 6 of the UAE Federal Law 6 stipulates that the articles and memorandum of association of each Islamic bank and each Islamic investment company authorised to conduct business in the UAE should provide for the appointment of a *Shari'ah* Supervisory Authority comprising at least three members. The articles of association of each institution should clearly indicate how the *Shari'ah* Authority should be formed, its terms of reference and an indication of how it should discharge its duties. This provision has been applied by all Islamic banks operating in the UAE including Dubai Islamic Bank, Abu Dhabi Islamic Bank, Sharjah Islamic Bank and Noor Islamic Bank. Article 6 states that the names of nominated members of each *Shari'ah* Supervisory Authority should be presented to the Higher *Shari'ah* Authority for approval, but as the Higher Authority does not yet exist, this provision remains redundant.

Article 7 states that Islamic banks and investment companies shall be subject to state audit but that the State Audit Bureau can only act after an audit and cannot interfere with work in progress or challenge their policies. This seems to give a substantial degree of latitude to Islamic banks and investment companies and challenges the usefulness of their accountability. In some respects, although the legal framework governing Islamic banking and finance in the UAE is well intentioned, it raises more questions than it answers.

Additions to the Central Bank of Kuwait Law to provide for the regulation of Islamic banking

The law providing for the establishment of the Central Bank of Kuwait and its regulation of the banking system was passed in 1968. When the Kuwait Finance House (KFH) was established in 1977 as the first Islamic bank in the country it was exempted from the banking regulations as it was deemed not to be a bank. The Ministry of Finance had a minority stake in the equity of KFH as a political symbol of the government's support and it was therefore to exercise regulatory responsibilities rather than the Central Bank. This arrangement prevailed until 2003 by which time KFH had become a major financial institution, not only in Kuwait, but globally, as it was the second-largest stock-market-listed Islamic financial institution worldwide after Al Rajhi Bank of Saudi Arabia.

The Ministry of Finance never performed normal regulatory functions as it was not equipped to play such a role, hence KFH enjoyed considerable freedom to develop its business as it saw fit. It became the leading institution in Kuwait for real-estate finance and its retail-banking business included a major share in vehicle finance. There were, however, criticisms from the other banks that its activities constituted unfair competition and some concern from customers concerning the monopoly it enjoyed in Islamic banking in Kuwait. In response to these criticisms and reservations by the Central Bank of Kuwait about possible systemic risks, the government of Kuwait decided that KFH should come under the authority of the Central Bank and that the 1968 Law should be amended and extended to make provision for Islamic banking.[4]

Subsequently, in 2003, an additional section, number 10, was included in the Banking Law to specifically make provision for Islamic banking. The legislation was not only designed to provide regulatory provision for KFH but also to allow other entrants to establish Islamic banks. Subsequently, Boubyan Bank was established and the Kuwait Real Estate Bank converted all its operations into being *Shari'ah* compliant and was renamed Kuwait International Bank. As the legislative changes were introduced rather late, Kuwait had the advantage of being able to draw on the experiences of other jurisdictions as well as the work conducted by the Accounting and Auditing Organisation for Islamic Financial Services (AAOIFI) and the Kuala Lumpur-based Islamic Financial Services Board (IFSB) where KFH has an Islamic banking subsidiary.

Section 10 of the Central Bank of Kuwait Law, although introduced as an amendment, is more comprehensive than most specifically Islamic banking laws. Article 86 of Section 10 outlines Islamic banking deposit and financing facilities including *murabaha, musharaka* and *mudaraba*. The Article clarifies the remit of Islamic banks by stressing that they conduct direct investment operations both on their own account and on behalf of their clients, including through partnership arrangements. Islamic banks can establish subsidiary companies or hold equity in existing companies and become directly involved in economic activity. In other words, they should not be classified as mere financial intermediaries like conventional banks. Article 86 also provides for foreign Islamic banks operating in Kuwait, although none have yet opened branches in the country. Rather, the direct investment has been outward, notably the activities of KFH in Turkey and Malaysia, which are regulated by the authorities in the host countries and not by the Central Bank of Kuwait.

While Article 86 recognised that Islamic banks often established subsidiary companies as part of their normal operations, Article 87 introduced restrictions on such activity. Each Islamic bank operating in Kuwait would henceforth only be allowed to establish one subsidiary company with a minimum capital of 15 million Kuwaiti Dinar (KD) of which the bank should have a majority shareholding of at least 51 per cent. This provision was to prevent Islamic banks establishing numerous small companies outside their control which, if they got into difficulties, could undermine the financial stability of the bank with potentially adverse consequences for bank depositors and the Central Bank of Kuwait if it was forced to intervene to inject new capital to keep the bank solvent.

Articles 88 to 92 concern the procedures for the establishment and registration of new Islamic banks which are similar to those for conventional banks with a minimum capital requirement of KD 75 million or KD 15 million in the case of a foreign Islamic bank establishing a branch in Kuwait. Founder shareholders should subscribe a minimum of 10 per cent of the capital, but not more than 20 per cent, to ensure diversity of ownership as concentration can result in conflicts of interest.

Under Article 93 each Islamic bank in Kuwait must have an independent *Shari'ah* Supervisory Board comprising at least three members appointed by the bank's general assembly in line with AAOIFI and IFSB recommendations. The memorandum of agreement and articles of association of each Islamic bank should specify how its *Shari'ah*

Supervisory Board is established and its powers and procedures. Where conflicts arise amongst members of a *Shari'ah* Supervisory Board that cannot be resolved internally, these can be referred to the *Fatwa* Board of the Ministry of *Awqaf* and Islamic Affairs. This body has the final authority, but this has never arisen in practice, which is fortunate as the *Fatwa* Board members have no specialised knowledge of *fiqh muamalat* pertaining to Islamic finance. Article 93 stipulates that the *Shari'ah* Supervisory Board should prepare an annual report of its opinions of the bank's operations which should be submitted to the General Assembly of shareholders and published in the Bank's annual report.

Article 94 gives the Central Bank authority to open accounts with Islamic banks and accept deposits from Islamic banks provided the terms of these facilities conforms with Islamic financial principles. Article 95 authorises the Central Bank to provide emergency funding for Islamic banks for a six-month period renewable for a further six-month maximum. It can also purchase and sell Islamic bank securities. All these operations and the instruments used should be in accordance with Islamic financial principles. The Central Bank can also issue instruments which conform to Islamic financial principles, notably *sukuk*, although these are not specifically cited in the Law. There have been a number of corporate *sukuk* issuances in Kuwait, but no sovereign *sukuk*.

Article 96 of the Central Bank of Kuwait Law distinguishes between the rights of current or sight depositors and investment depositors with Islamic banks. The former have the right to withdraw their funds on demand and have their deposits guaranteed with no liability for losses. Investment depositors participate in the Islamic banks profits and losses in proportion to their shares of total deposits. Therefore their deposits are not guaranteed and their capital is potentially at risk in a similar manner to equity investors.

In practice investment-account depositors have never suffered from capital losses in Kuwait, but if losses arise, under Article 96 there would be no obligation by the Central Bank of Kuwait to offer compensation.

Article 98 provides the Central Bank with considerable powers in regulating the business of Islamic banks but these are consistent with its powers over conventional banks. It can specify the maximum financing of a single project to avoid excessive concentration exposure, the maximum equity holdings and the maximum deposit the bank can accept from a single customer. Under Article 99 it is recognised that Islamic banks may own residential property to facilitate Islamic financial transactions such as *murabaha*, *ijara* and diminishing *musharaka*, but apart from these cases, as with conventional banks, the banks should not own private property unless it is used for business premises for a branch or staff accommodation, or acquired as a result of an unfulfilled obligation by a client.

Overall the addition to the Central Bank of Kuwait Law to accommodate Islamic banks represents an impressive piece of legislation. It seems to have achieved its purposes and it provides a template which could benefit other jurisdictions, not only in the GCC, but more widely where new laws governing Islamic finance are being considered.

United Kingdom law pertaining to Islamic finance

Any financial institution seeking to provide Islamic banking or other financial services in the United Kingdom has to apply for a licence under the Financial Services and Market Act of 2000. This covers the regulatory framework and the licensing requirements for all financial service activity as there is no separate legislation for the registration of Islamic financial services.[5] To obtain authorisation to conduct

business an Islamic financial institution has to be incorporated as a company in the United Kingdom and have its
head office and senior management in country. It must also
have adequate resources for the business it seeks to undertake and the management must fulfil fit and proper criteria,
in particular be able to undertake business in a sound and
proper manner without dependence on outsiders whose
interests are not declared.[6]

The applicant should consult with the Financial Services
Authority (FSA) about the products they intend to offer
in order that the appropriate regulatory requirements are
determined. For example, bank deposits will fall within the
remit of the deposit-protection scheme which can raise the
issue of guarantees for investment depositors. These issues
have to be addressed before such deposits are offered so
that depositors are aware of their rights and obligations.
Islamic banks cannot be exempted from deposit-protection
insurance and must contribute to the Financial Services
Protection Scheme whereby bank deposits of up to £85,000
are fully protected. For *mudaraba* investment-account
holders the guarantee must be offered, but they can sign
wavers indicating that they do not require protection so that
their deposit contracts are *Shari'ah* compliant.

The FSA as a secular authority is not concerned with
what is *Shari'ah* compliant, but in the interests of customer
protection they need assurance that if products and services
offered purport to be *Shari'ah* compliant, then there should
be some creditable system in place to ensure that this is the
case. The expectation of the FSA is that the Islamic bank or
financial service provider will appoint a *Shari'ah* supervisory board, and it will be concerned about how the *Shari'ah*
supervisory board affects the running of the institution, and
in particular whether its role is merely advisory or if it has
an executive function.

The five Islamic banks operating in the United Kingdom have argued that their *Shari'ah* supervisory boards have an advisory rather than an executive role and this has been accepted by the FSA. If their role was designated to be executive their status would be that of company directors who in the case of the United Kingdom have to meet fit and proper criteria. One limitation on executive directors is that they can only serve on one board, as if they were executives in two or more companies then conflicts of interest would inevitably arise and there could be confidentiality issues. As the *Shari'ah* scholars who serve on the supervisory boards of Islamic banks in the United Kingdom serve on multiple boards they would be disqualified under fit and proper criteria if they were designated as playing an executive role. Nevertheless, although designating their role as advisory meets the regulatory requirements, it raises wider issues. The *fatwa* of the *Shari'ah* supervisory board are supposed to be mandatory as if the Islamic financial institution rejected their rulings it would no longer be *Shari'ah* compliant. In contrast, an advisory role means just that, there being no compulsion to follow the advice.

In the interests of consumer protection the FSA is also concerned with promotional and marketing material used by Islamic banks. The requirement is that it should be clear, fair and not misleading. Given the complexity of many Islamic financial products and the misunderstandings of some clients and potential clients, especially by those for whom English, and indeed Arabic, are second languages, this provision is especially important.

Tax treatment of Islamic financial contracts

In the GCC there are no tax issues that arise with Islamic financial products given the absence of income tax, transfer taxes and capital gains tax, most government revenue coming from oil and gas revenue. In Malaysia tax issues arise, but there have been many exemptions for Islamic financial products as part of the government's effort to make the country a hub for Islamic finance. Its experience is not reviewed here, but rather that of the United Kingdom, which has more applicability to other jurisdictions where the aim is to create a level playing field for Islamic finance rather than discriminating against it or providing special favours.[7]

The particular issue that arose in the United Kingdom was the stamp duty payable on Islamic mortgages as with the *murabaha* structure which was first used the Islamic bank purchasing the property would be liable for stamp duty and the client would also be liable for stamp duty when they acquired the property from the bank.[8] As property prices have increased in the United Kingdom, especially in London and the South East, stamp duty, which is based on the value of the property, has become especially burdensome. Having a double liability made Islamic mortgages unattractive and unviable.

Following lobbying by the banks that wished to provide Islamic mortgages in the United Kingdom and the Muslim Council of Britain, the government agreed to introduce legislative changes under the 2004 Finance Act which would enable *murabaha* financing of residential property to be treated as a single transaction and therefore there would only be liability for stamp duty by the client, not by the Islamic bank. As a consequence the mortgage costs became significantly lower. Subsequently, however, many in the Islamic finance industry argued that *murabaha* was unsuitable for residential mortgages as it was short term and inflexible, as the markup was fixed when the transaction was agreed and bore little relation to the Islamic bank's cost of funding. Therefore *ijara* was more suitable, but this entailed more legislation.

Subsequently, under the Finance Act of 2007, *ijara* mortgages were designated as Home Purchase Plans under which only a single amount of stamp duty was payable.[9] This designation was then applied to diminishing *musharaka* mortgages involving a partnership agreement between the Islamic bank and the home buyer. This has become the most popular form of Islamic housing finance in the United Kingdom as the terms are flexible with provision for lower payments during the early years of the contract.

Legislative issues pertaining to *takaful* will be discussed in Chapter 8 and those relating to *sukuk* in Chapter 9. Often provision for Islamic finance can be made at the regulatory level, however, without the need for legislation. The regulation of Islamic banks is the subject of the next chapter.

Notes

1. Rodney Wilson, 'Islam and Malaysia's economic development', *Journal of Islamic Studies*, 9: 2, 1998, pp. 259–76.
2. Laws of Malaysia, *Islamic Banking Act*, Law Number 276 (1983; reprinted Kuala Lumpur, 2001), pp. 5–9.
3. UAE Federal Law No. 6, *Regarding Islamic Banks, Financial Institutions and Investment Companies* (Abu Dhabi, 1985).
4. Rodney Wilson, 'Approaches to Islamic banking in the Gulf', in Eckart Woertz (ed.), *Gulf Financial Markets* (Dubai: Gulf Research Centre, 2011), pp. 221–38.
5. Michael Ainley, Ali Mashayekhi, Robert Hicks, Arshadur Rahman and Ali Ravalia, *Islamic Finance in the UK: Regulation and Challenges* (London: Financial Services Authority, 2007), pp. 10–15.
6. Rodney Wilson, 'Islamic banking in the United Kingdom', in M. Fahim Khan and Mario Porzio (eds), *Islamic Banking in Europe* (Cheltenham: Edward Elgar, 2010), pp. 212–21.

7. Mohammed Amin, 'Taxation of Islamic financial products', in Humayon A. Dar and Umar F. Moghul (eds), *The Chancellor Guide to the Legal and Shari'a Aspects of Islamic Finance* (London: Chancellor Publications, 2009), pp. 77–104.
8. For a survey of Islamic home finance in the United Kingdom, see Elaine Housby, *Islamic Financial Services in the United Kingdom* (Edinburgh: Edinburgh University Press, 2011), pp. 81–106.
9. HM Treasury, *The Development of Islamic Finance in the United Kingdom: the Government Perspective* (London: HM Treasury, 2008), pp. 16–17.

CHAPTER 7
REGULATION OF ISLAMIC BANKS

Most of the adaptation necessary for Islamic banks to function has been undertaken at the regulatory level rather than through legislation. This is less politically controversial as changes can be introduced, many of which are technical in nature, often without those who might be opposed realising the significance of what is happening. Regulators are, of course, accountable for their actions to government, but they are not subject to direct questions from special interest groups and the general public in the same way as legislators. Indeed many regulators enjoy a considerable degree of autonomy, as although in the long run they may be accountable for their actions, in the short run they have considerable discretion both over what information is required from the institutions they regulate and how often reporting should occur.

The worldwide trend towards deregulation over the two decades prior to the global financial crisis was undoubtedly helpful for Islamic banks as it enabled them to introduce a wider range of deposits and financing instruments without too many questions being asked. Less scrutiny can be helpful for product innovation whereas tighter scrutiny may result in less willingness to change the status quo. Since the crisis of 2008, the move to tighter regulation poses challenges for Islamic banks which in the long run may discourage innovation. As was seen in the previous chapter, the Financial Services Authority in the United Kingdom takes an interest in what Islamic financial products are offered, but there has been less interest at this level by regulators in the GCC. It is, however, likely that such information will be sought in the future as dissatisfied clients of Islamic banks become more willing to take legal action.

Financial regulators have two major objectives, the first being that the institutions they regulate should stay solvent and, secondly, that the clients of the regulated institutions have access to relevant information so that they can effectively manage their financial affairs. The latter refers to product information but it is the former that has received most attention from regulators of both conventional and Islamic banks in the Muslim world. Remaining solvent means having adequate liquidity, which poses problems for Islamic banks which cannot hold interest-bearing treasury bills or maintain deposits with central banks that pay interest. If the alternative is simply holding non-interest deposits with central banks the result is Islamic banks being at a competitive disadvantage to conventional banks. Hence, there will be special pleading to hold less liquidity and to management liquidity risk in other ways. How regulators respond to such demands varies across jurisdictions and may ultimately depend on wider factors such as political support for Islamic banking, even though regulators are supposed to be apolitical.

These issues are best addressed in specific context, and therefore in this chapter the relevant guiding principles of the Islamic Financial Services Board (IFSB) are reviewed. This is the institution that provides guidance to regulators worldwide on how they should accommodate Islamic financial institutions. The regulations of Bank Indonesia concerning Islamic banking are then examined, this being the Central Bank of the world's most populous Muslim country where at present Islamic finance is a niche activity, but with considerable potential to grow. Then the regulations of the Central Bank of Bahrain are reviewed followed by those of the Qatar Central Bank, the Qatar Financial Centre and the Dubai International Financial Centre. This will enable the reader to contrast the approach to Islamic bank regulation in South East Asia with that in the Gulf.

The Islamic Financial Services Board (IFSB) guidelines on risk management

The IFSB is a young institution that was inaugurated in 2002 and started its work the following year. It is a Kuala Lumpur-based standards-setting authority but with an international remit as the body which provides guidelines to central banks and other authorities on good practice in the regulation of Islamic financial institutions. Its role is recognised by the International Monetary Fund and the Bank for International Settlements which is responsible for the Basel standards which are supported by the G20 leading economies. It has provided guiding principles on risk management, capital adequacy, transparency and corporate governance. These include separate documents for regulators of Islamic banks, *takaful* operators, *sukuk* and collective investment schemes. *Takaful* is covered in the next chapter, *sukuk* in Chapter 9 and collective investment schemes in Chapter 10. Here, the guiding principles pertaining to the regulation of Islamic banks are considered.

When drafting its standards the IFSB is not starting from a blank sheet of paper, but rather has to take account of the international standards for banking regulation under Basel I and II, and in due course Basel III. Its approach is similar to that of the Accounting and Auditing Organisation for

Islamic Financial Services (AAOIFI) when setting standards on financial reporting. AAOIFI aims to complement and indeed enhance the International Financial Reporting Standards (IFRS) by applying these to Islamic banks. The aim of both the AAOIFI and IFSB is not to provide substitute or alternative standards but rather to accept the existing international framework.

The first standard which the IFSB instigated in 2005 was on risk management.[1] The risk management framework was identical to that for conventional banks with credit risk, equity risk, market risk, liquidity risk, rate of return risk and operational risks considered in separate chapters. The only headline change was the replacement of interest-rate risk by rate-of-return risk. The requirements for managing credit risk were the same as for conventional banks as this involved having a strategy for risk mitigation, performing due diligence reviews and having a methodology for the measurement and management of credit exposures. The main distinctive feature was that an Islamic bank's risk management strategy should take account of the appropriate steps to comply with *Shari'ah* rules and principles.

However, the unique features of Islamic bank assets and liabilities are apparent when they are analysed from a risk management perspective. For example, during the life of a *murabaha* contract the market risk associated with the trading transaction is transformed into credit risk. Similarly, the capital invested in a *mudaraba* or *musharaka* contract which could be classified as equity is transformed into debt in the case of proven misconduct by the *mudarab* or *musharaka* managing partner.

Credit risk

The management of credit risk poses challenges for Islamic banks as they cannot levy and profit from additional

charges in the case of payments not being made by counterparties. This creates potential moral hazard problems as
if a defaulter is in debt to both an Islamic and a conventional bank they may choose to give priority to settling the
conventional debt obligation in order to avoid paying additional interest. An Islamic bank can obviously not charge
interest, but they can levy a late payment fee which can be
donated to charity so that the bank does not profit itself
from the increased indebtedness, which would be morally
unjust. The IFSB states that Islamic banks may, at their
discretion, provide a rebate for counterparties that settle
their obligations early.[2] Such a discount cannot be stated
in the contract as the *Shari'ah* board is unlikely to approve
it. Informal understandings are unlikely to be appealing to
Islamic bank clients, however, and could be perceived as
simply a way to circumvent the *Shari'ah* board.

Equity investment risk

In their guidelines on equity investment risk involving
mudaraba and *musharaka* contracts the IFSB recommends
that the risks of the *mudarib* or *musharaka* partners as
counterparties should be assessed. If they get into financial difficulties this may have implications for their partners, especially if they wish to sell out to meet their financial
obligations. If the *mudaraba* or *musharaka* arrangement
involves the establishment of a special purpose vehicle
(SPV) as a limited liability company this may mitigate some
of the risks as the creditors of the distressed partners will
not have recourse to the assets held by the SPV. These issues
are not raised by the IFSB but it is clear that in the case of
mudaraba and *musharaka* there should be a due diligence
review of the contractual arrangements and the liabilities
and obligations of the partners.

The IFSB stresses that because of a lack of information

in partnerships through *mudaraba* and *musharaka* contracts, the investors may need to get actively involved in management themselves or at least take an active interest in business developments. The analogy is with private-equity investment where the venture capitalists often take a hands-on approach. As the major investment risks often arise with termination the IFSB recommends that Islamic financial institutions should define and establish the exit strategy with respect to equity investments including the extension and redemption conditions for *mudaraba* and *musharaka*. It is beyond the remit of the IFSB to define the exit strategy which will depend on the particular circumstances of the investment, but it indicates that the strategy should be approved by the *Shari'ah* board which may have views about whether the nominal value of the invested capital should be repaid or if the market value of the assets should determine the amount of capital returned.

Market risk

Market risk is more broadly defined than equity investment risk by the IFSB, as it arises in debt-based contracts and not only with equity arrangements. In the case of *murabaha*, for example, the market value of the assets being financed may vary and unless the buying and selling are undertaken simultaneously an Islamic bank will be exposed to market risk. Similarly, with *ijara* contracts the owner is exposed to market risk on the residual value of the leased assets at the end of the lease period, or the value of the assets at the time of a default by the lessee if such an unfortunate event occurs. *Salam* also involves market risk as the financier is taking a long position by paying in full for a commodity in advance as the spot price will be subject to short-term fluctuations, the effect of which will be to make the long position profitable or loss making. In all of these cases the IFSB recommends that the Islamic financial institution should define its risk appetite and ensure it has sufficient paid-up capital to cover these risks.[3]

Liquidity risk-management issues

The IFSB first addressed the issue of liquidity risk management in its Guiding Principles in 2005, but its approach has been developed further in Exposure Draft 12 issued in October 2011, which is scheduled to become a standard from 2012 after a period of public consultation.[4] In the 2005 document the IFSB recommended that the liquidity management framework of Islamic banks should take account of their distinctive exposures to current-account depositors, those with unrestricted *mudaraba* deposits and those with restricted *mudaraba* deposits. In the case of current-account depositors there would have to be sufficient funds available to meet all likely demands, but the *mudaraba* investment-account deposits were subject to periods of notice for withdrawals, hence reducing immediate liquidity requirements. The 2005 IFSB Guiding Principles were silent on the type of liquid asset to be held, the main stress being on exposure and cash-flow management and the control of exposure mismatches.

Exposure Draft 12 on liquidity management contains much more detail on the responsibilities of Islamic banks and their regulators in measuring and managing liquidity risk. As with the Basel standards the emphasis is on measuring and forecasting cash flows although no time horizons are specified for the forecast periods. A more sophisticated approach is advocated than in the 2005 document as Islamic banks are expected to model the behavioural profile of *mudaraba* investment-account holders, especially those with unrestricted accounts, and estimate through stress testing how that behaviour may be affected by adverse financial developments resulting from banking or economic crises. Maturity gap analysis is advocated as a tool for liquidity management as if the gap between demand and short-term deposits and longer-term financing is increasing then this has implications for the precautionary reserves which are usually maintained in the form of liquid assets.[5]

There has been a trend for maturity gaps to increase worldwide as Islamic banks have provided more *ijara* and *istisna'a* funding rather than short-term *murabaha*. Although welcome by clients from a financing perspective, and as a means of increasing returns which benefits shareholders, widening maturity gaps inevitably mean higher risks. A gradual increase in maturity gaps can be justified as this allows time for Islamic banks to develop a strategy for the additional liquidity management which will be necessary. A sudden widening of maturity gaps and an overdependence on short-term interbank financing to cover asset positions could be viewed as potentially reckless, with a strong possibility of insolvency occurring.

The IFSB addresses the issues of both the categorisation and the composition of liquid assets. Islamic banks have to hold liquid assets in the minimum amounts or proportions specified by their regulators, but in addition maintain profit-equalisation reserves which are used to maintain profit payouts to *mudaraba* investment-account holders. As these reserves are designated for this particular purpose they cannot count towards general reserve requirements, although the fact that they exist may encourage depositors to maintain their deposits with the bank therefore limiting the liquidity requirements associated with sudden deposit drawdown. One issue facing Islamic banks, which is not discussed by the IFSB, is that often depositors have other current accounts with conventional banks into which their salaries are paid. Their Islamic bank accounts are regarded as savings vehicles rather than for covering current expenses. The balances in the current account tend to move in a predictable manner over a monthly payments cycle. In contrast, although the velocity of circulation is much lower with investment *mudaraba* deposits, withdrawals tend to be larger and less predictable, as for example when a saver is accumulating funds in the account to acquire a vehicle and then empties the account when the purchase is made.[6]

The composition of liquidity for Islamic banks, or in other words what liquid assets are available to hold, poses a particular challenge. As interest-bearing treasury bills were precluded as not being *Shari'ah* compliant, much reliance was placed on *murabaha*-based contracts for the purchase and sale of commodities. Liquid deposit facilities were offered by banks in London, as discussed in Chapter 3, using a *murabaha* structure with the underlying transactions being undertaken on the London Metal Exchange. The banks offering these facilities were conventional, but appointed *Shari'ah* scholars to approve the structures. Such liquidity placements involve significant legal structuring costs reducing the returns paid to the Islamic financial institutions.

Other products cited in the IFSB Exposure Draft on Liquidity include interbank *mudaraba* and *wakala* placements. The IFSB Draft draws attention to the risks and potential volatility of the latter, which means its suitability as a vehicle for liquid funds must be questionable.[7] *Mudaraba* deposits would seem to be a safer option provided there is not systemic risk engulfing both the Islamic bank making the deposit placements and the bank accepting the deposits.

Short-term *sukuk* are potentially the most appropriate instrument for liquidity holdings. In Chapter 9 the many *sukuk* structures and contracts available will be reviewed. For liquidity purposes 90-day or 180-day *sukuk* based on

salam structures have been used in Bahrain. These, however, are not tradable under *Shari'ah* rules as the commodity on which the *sukuk* is based is only available at the end
of the *salam* transaction. Under *Shari'ah* a commodity must
be in possession of the seller before it can be traded as otherwise if there is a delivery problem the contract cannot be
honoured. *Ijara* contracts may be more suitable as the good,
equipment or property, the income from which provides
the *sukuk* yield, is already in the possession of the seller.
In practice, however, although in Malaysia such *sukuk* are
widely acquired for treasury purposes as there is a developed market, elsewhere *sukuk* markets are underdeveloped.
This results in *sukuk* holdings being illiquid and therefore
unsuitable for use for reserve purposes.

Operational risk and rate-of-return risk

The IFSB Risk Management Guiding Principles cover operational risk which includes risk associated with a break-
down of Information Technology (IT) systems and fraud
and other misdemeanours of bank staff. The operational
risks associated with IT systems are no different for Islamic
banks than for conventional banks, although as the former
are smaller in size and have more limited technical capability much of the specialised work is outsourced. Such
contracting out has advantages and disadvantages from a
risk management perspective, the potential problem being
communications with the firm undertaking the work. The
advantage, however, is that if there are failures, another firm
may be given the contract, a possibility which encourages
technical sub-contractors to perform.

Fraud can arise in Islamic banks as in their conventional
equivalents, and regulators need to ensure adequate recruitment and management control systems are in place. The
religious and cultural ethos of Islamic banks arguably makes

fraud less likely, and although there have been some high-profile cases involving junior managers, the low incidence of fraud over the last four decades is encouraging.

Rate-of-return risk is the same as interest-rate risk, and therefore it might be assumed that this does not arise in the case of Islamic banks. However, the returns paid by Islamic banks to *mudaraba* investment depositors have to be kept competitive with those of savings accounts with conventional banks. Hence, when interest rates rise, Islamic bank profit payouts also increase, with adverse implications for the costs of funding. However, as the returns for existing *murabaha* financing contracts cannot rise, in the short term Islamic bank profit margins are squeezed, a situation that will only be rectified with new *murabaha* contracts with greater markups between buying and selling prices. This phenomenon is referred to by the IFSB as displaced commercial risk. Regulators need to monitor these developments to ensure the Islamic bank operations under their ambit remain viable.

Bank Indonesia regulation

Having considered the international guidelines on Islamic banking regulation from the IFSB it is instructive to examine national regulations, starting with Indonesia, the world's most populous Muslim country. Islamic banking was relatively late to be introduced into Indonesia, the first institution, Bank Muamalat, opening for business in 1992. Islamic banking has expanded rapidly since then, with twenty-six Islamic banks competing for business, but most of the institutions remain small with the assets of Bank Muamalat being worth less than $2 billion and half the Islamic banks having assets worth less than $100 million.[8] There is, however, much support for Islamic finance from people of modest means and it is estimated that Islamic banks have attracted over 16 per cent of total savings in Indonesia.[9]

Banking legislation enacted in 1999 governs the working of Bank Indonesia, the Central Bank which regulates all banking in Indonesia, both conventional and Islamic.[10] Chapter 6 Articles 24 to 35 provides for the regulation of banks, but there was no special provision for Islamic banks in the legislation, indeed they were not referred to in the 1999 Act. The provisions were, however, amended in 2004 to permit Bank Indonesia to make funds available to Islamic banks for a ninety-day period, with this temporary funding being *Shari'ah* compliant.[11] This amendment was elaborated further following the global financial crisis of 2008 when a number of small Islamic banks that had obtained ninety-day funding from Bank Indonesia were unable to repay. Hence, in 2009 provision was made for Bank Indonesia to dispose of the collateral under its control provided by the banks seeking funding which could no longer meet their obligations. A definition of what constituted acceptable collateral was provided, with reference being made to high-quality marketable collateral.[12]

Although at the legislative level provision was made for Bank Indonesia's role as lender of the last resort with respect to Islamic banks, there was no distinctive provision for their governance taking account of the *Shari'ah*-compliant nature of their operations. This has been dealt with at the regulatory level in Indonesia, with comprehensive measures introduced in 2009.[13] The regulations concern the requirements when commercial banks are converted to becoming Islamic banks, but also apply to existing Islamic banks. The 2009 regulations encompass the regulatory provisions of the previous year on *Shari'ah* bank products and the establishment of *Shari'ah* banking committees.

In the regulations a distinction is made between *Shari'ah* commercial banks which provide payments services and *Shari'ah* rural banks which do not. The former are required to be capitalised and adhere to the same reporting standards as conventional commercial banks, the minimum capital being 8 per cent of total assets, whereas there are lower capitalisation requirements for the *Shari'ah* rural banks in line with those for other rural banks. The *Shari'ah* principles under which both types of banks operate are determined by a National *Shari'ah* Board, the Indonesia Council of *Ulama*, which is appointed by and is accountable to the Governors of Bank Indonesia. Under Article 2 conventional banks can convert into being *Shari'ah* banks but Article 3 precludes this being reversed.

The procedures for the conversion to a *Shari'ah* bank are spelt out in the regulations including the changes to the articles of association and the use of the 'Ib' logo designating Islamic banks which signifies that the bank's operations are approved by the National *Shari'ah* Board. This is to provide client assurance in the regulated institution and ensure there is centralised control. Institutions purporting to be Islamic, but which are unregulated, cannot use the logo. Banks licensed as Islamic should have all their new operations *Shari'ah* compliant sixty days before the licence is granted. They are subsequently allowed up to one year to settle all their conventional business undertaken prior to the conversion date.[14]

Bahrain's Islamic banking regulations

Bahrain has functioned as a regional financial centre since 1976, keeping its market open to foreign banks, while Saudi Arabia and Kuwait only licensed majority locally owned institutions. Bahrain has more Islamic financial institutions than any other centre, with twenty-four Islamic banks and eleven Islamic *takaful* insurance companies, most of which serve the regional rather than the local market.[15] It is very dependent on Saudi business, however, and as the latter opens up its financial sector, there are competitive challenges to Bahrain, including in Islamic banking.

The Bahrain Monetary Agency, now renamed as the Central Bank of Bahrain, has been very active in promoting Bahrain as an Islamic financial centre. The island has been the headquarters of AAOIFI since its foundation in 1991, which serves as the standard-setting body for financial reporting.[16] Most Islamic financial institutions worldwide are members of AAOIFI and many adhere to its standards, which build on rather than replace the International Financial Reporting Standards (IFRS) used by most conventional banks in Europe and Asia.

Bahrain also hosts the International Islamic Financial Market (IIFM) whose remit is to help Islamic capital and money markets through promoting common trading standards.[17] Its work is at an early stage, but it has support from the central banks of Bahrain, Brunei, Indonesia, Malaysia and the Sudan, as well as from the Jeddah-based Islamic Development Bank. However, the central banks of other GCC countries are not members, preferring to focus their efforts on their own markets and institutions. The Bahrain-based Liquidity Management Centre has also been slow to take off, its aim being to facilitate the placement of surplus funds of Islamic financial institutions into profitable traded instruments.[18] The capital was subscribed by Kuwait Finance House, Bahrain and Dubai Islamic Banks and the Islamic Development Bank, but they have used international investment banks for much of their own *sukuk* issuance rather than the Liquidity Management Centre. The other major role of the Liquidity Management Centre is to promote secondary market trading of *sukuk*. Trading volumes have been limited however, with eleven buying and selling transactions in 2005, twenty-five in 2006 and only fifteen in 2007. No more up-to-date figures have been released.

The Central Bank of Bahrain has a detailed rulebook which governs all financial activity on the island, including Islamic banking. However, there are only two additional specific requirements for Islamic banks; that each Islamic bank must have an independent *Shari'ah* supervisory committee and that Islamic banks should adopt the AAOIFI standards for their financial reporting.[19]

It is debatable how far Bahrain's relative success in attracting Islamic financial institutions is due to a pull factor, the encouragement of the Central Bank of Bahrain, or a push factor, the unwillingness of its neighbours to grant new licences to Islamic banks and *takaful* insurance operators in the past. There are six Islamic retail banks catering for the local market in Bahrain, including Bahrain Islamic Bank and Shamil Bank, now renamed and re-launched as Ithmaar Bank, but these are all small financial institutions. Their sustainability in the long term is open to question, especially as Saudi Arabia has opened up its market for financial services since 2005 as a condition of its World Trade Organization membership, although admittedly the nine new entrants, which include Deutsche Bank, BNP Parisbas and J. P. Morgan Chase, have only a limited interest in Islamic finance. The position of Bahrain as an international centre for Islamic banking has not been helped by the unrest following the events of the Arab Spring. Although there have been no withdrawals from the market new investment does not appear to be forthcoming because of political risk perceptions.

The Qatar regulatory environment

Unlike Bahrain, Qatar and Dubai have established financial centres in free zones which are governed by their own laws and regulations based on English Common Law as applied to finance. Both the Qatar Financial Centre and the Dubai International Financial Centre (DIFC) are separate jurisdictions with disputes not subject to the civil law which applies outside the zones in Qatar and the UAE. Institutions functioning in the free zones are also outside the jurisdiction of the local *Shari'ah* courts, although admittedly *Shari'ah* arbitration is rarely used in banking disputes, the *Shari'ah* court remit being largely confined to disputes within families over matters such as inheritance.

The Qatar Financial Centre has a detailed rulebook covering Islamic finance, including criteria for *Shari'ah* supervision.[20] A higher proportion of bank deposits are *Shari'ah* compliant in Qatar than in any other GCC state but institutions such as the Qatar Islamic Bank, Masraf Al Rayan and the Qatar International Islamic Bank focus on the domestic market, and despite the international designation of the last, it is regulated by the Qatar Central Bank rather than by the financial centre authority. The merits of a division of regulatory responsibilities in a small state such as Qatar can be questioned, and in July 2007 the government recognised this by signalling that it intended to establish a single regulatory authority although this has still not been introduced.

The major commercial banks in Qatar have established Islamic affiliates, most notably the Qatar National Bank which has an Al Islami subsidiary and the Commercial Bank of Qatar with its Al Safa Islamic Banking subsidiary and Doha Bank Islamic.[21] This increasing competition in a relatively small market encouraged Qatar's Islamic banks to look overseas for diversification and expansion. The Qatar

Islamic Bank owns the London-based European Finance House and the Kuala Lumpur-based Asian Finance Bank. It also has subsidiaries in Lebanon, Bahrain, Yemen and Kazakhstan operating under its own name, and is undertaking feasibility studies of the Turkish, Egyptian and Indonesian markets. Masraf Al Rayan has established a consumer-financing operation in Saudi Arabia and is seeking permission to open a branch in Libya, a wholly Muslim country with no Islamic banks to date.

The decision taken by the Qatar Central Bank in 2011 to no longer allow conventional banks to provide Islamic financial services is having major implications for the Islamic banking sector in Qatar. The position of the Qatar Islamic Bank has been strengthened especially with the closure of Qatar National Bank's Al Islami subsidiary. There has been some account migration to Qatar Islamic Bank as depositors with *Shari'ah*-compliant accounts have not wanted to see their accounts reverting to become conventional.

Islamic banking regulation in Dubai

The introduction of a single regulatory system in the UAE is unlikely, as the country is a federation in which each emirate enjoys considerable autonomy, although the Central Bank oversees the entire banking system with the exception of banks registered with the DIFC. The latter has the highest international profile in the region, and Islamic finance is becoming increasingly significant for its interests. The DIFC has an Islamic Finance Advisory Council and has produced a detailed *Guide to Islamic Finance*. The DIFC has also produced a *Tailored Handbook for Islamic Banking*, but this mostly reproduces its general regulations. Its Islamic finance rules apply to both fully fledged Islamic banks and those with Islamic windows. One interesting provision is that profits-sharing investment accounts are not treated as investments but rather as deposit facilities.[22] The regulations specify that each institution offering Islamic financial services should appoint a *Shari'ah* board with at least three members.[23] Institutions are required to maintain records of the assessment of competency of *Shari'ah* board members for at least six years and highlight any conflicts of interest. The rulings are consistent with those of AAOIFI which is explicitly referred to.

As in Qatar, in the UAE the major Islamic banks are focused on the domestic market, indeed the Dubai and Abu Dhabi Islamic Banks largely concentrate on their home Emirates although they have branch networks throughout the UAE. The UAE market for Islamic banking has become overcrowded with new entrants, as the National Bank of Sharjah converted to being Sharjah Islamic Bank, while in Dubai Noor Islamic Bank was established in 2008 with one quarter of its capital subscribed by the government of Dubai and a further quarter by the ruler himself, Sheikh Mohammed bin Rashid Al Maktoum.[24] '*Noor*' means 'light' in Arabic, the aim being to be a high profile regional force in Islamic finance at the centre of attention. In reality, however, its main focus is on personal finance and credit cards, indicating it is yet another consumer-finance institution, its most distinctive plan to date being to establish a subsidiary in the Maldives through a joint venture.[25]

Competition can, of course, be helpful to financial development, but the emergence of rival centres in the Gulf has fragmented the Islamic finance industry and resulted in many very small institutions being licensed which cannot benefit from economies of scale or scope. None of the Islamic banks in the Gulf is in the top 100 world banks in terms of assets, and as a consequence, it is the major international banks such as HSBC, Deutsche Bank and Citibank that have moved into Islamic finance to fill the void, especially in investment banking, where capacity and capability are of critical importance. Although HSBC has based much of its Islamic banking operations in Dubai, the other investment banks conduct their Islamic finance business from London, where it is easier to recruit skilled professionals, rather than the GCC. The Financial Services Authority in the United Kingdom has made considerable efforts to accommodate Islamic banking within a conventional regulatory framework, providing a model which regulators in the GCC can in most respects follow. However, the United Kingdom policy of guaranteeing investment deposits, while putting the onus on depositors to ensure *Shari'ah* compliance by voluntarily giving up their right to deposit protection, is unlikely to be acceptable in the GCC.

Notes

1. Islamic Financial Services Board, *Guiding Principles of Risk Management for Institutions (Other than Insurance Institutions) Offering Only Islamic Financial Services*, Number 1, Kuala Lumpur, December 2005.
2. Ibid. paragraph 39, p. 10.
3. Ibid. paragraph 75, p. 17.
4. Islamic Financial Services Board, *Guiding Principles on Liquidity Risk Management for Institutions Offering Islamic Financial Services (Excluding Islamic Insurance and Islamic Collective Investment Schemes)*, Exposure Draft 12, Kuala Lumpur, October 2011.
5. Ibid. paragraph 61, p. 22.
6. Rodney Wilson and Remali Yusoff, 'An econometric analysis of conventional and Islamic bank deposits in Malaysia', *Review of Islamic Economics*, 9: 1, 2005, pp. 31–49.
7. Islamic Financial Services Board, *Guiding Principles on*

Liquidity Risk Management for Institutions Offering Islamic Financial Services (Excluding Islamic Insurance and Islamic Collective Investment Schemes), Exposure Draft 12, Kuala Lumpur, October 2011, paragraph 76, p. 26.

8. *The Banker*, 'Top 500 Islamic financial institutions', London, November 2010, p. 54.

9. Bank Indonesia, *Grand Strategy of Islamic Banking Market Development, Directorate of Islamic Banking*, Jakarta, July 2008, p. 21.

10. Bank Indonesia, *Act of the Republic of Indonesia Concerning Bank Indonesia*, Number 23, Jakarta, 1999.

11. Bank Indonesia, *Amendment to Act Number 23 of 1999 of the Republic of Indonesia Concerning Bank Indonesia*, Number 3, Jakarta, 2004, Article 11 clauses 1 and 2.

12. Bank Indonesia, *Second Amendment to Act Number 23 of 1999 of the Republic of Indonesia Concerning Bank Indonesia*, Number 6, Jakarta, 2009, Article 2 paragraphs 1 and 2.

13. Bank Indonesia, *Regulation Concerning the Conversion of Business Activities from Commercial to Shari'ah Banking*, Number 11/15, Jakarta, 2009.

14. Ibid. Article 17 (1) and Article 18.

15. 'Business Friendly Bahrain', *Islamic Financial Services*: www.bahrainfs.com/FSInBahrainIslamicFinance.aspx.

16. www.aaoifi.com.

17. www.iifm.net.

18. www.lmcbahrain.com.

19. Central Bank of Bahrain, *Rulebook*, Vol. 2, Islamic Banks, HC-1.3.15 and HC-1.3.16.

20. Qatar Financial Centre, *Rulebook on Islamic Finance*, Doha, 2005, pp. 1–22.

21. Oxford Business Group, 'Islamic financial services overview', *Report on Qatar* (Oxford: Oxford Business Group, 2008), pp. 64–6.

22. Dubai Financial Services Authority, *Islamic Finance Regulation*, Number 2.4.4–2.4.5, Dubai, 2010.

23. Ibid. Number 3.5.1.

24. Oxford Business Group, 'Lighting the way: Islamic financial services overview', *Report on Dubai* (Oxford: Oxford Business Group, 2008), pp. 96–7.

25. www.noorbank.com/.

CHAPTER 8
LAWS AND REGULATIONS FOR *TAKAFUL* OPERATORS AND PARTICIPANTS

Takaful developments have tended to lag behind those of Islamic banking at the operational, legal and regulatory levels. The aim of this chapter is to highlight the differences between *takaful* and conventional insurance contracts and discuss the relative merits of the different *takaful* structures, namely those based on *wakala* and *mudaraba* contracts. There has been relatively little legislation on *takaful*, the Malaysian Law of 1984 being the pioneering act. Much more detailed guidelines were issued in Malaysia in 2011 clarifying many of the issues, and these are cited here. Contrasts are drawn with the regulations in Bahrain for *takaful*, the most comprehensive in the Gulf. Reference will also be made to the Islamic Financial Services Board (IFSB) *Guiding Principles on* Takaful *Governance* and their more recent *Solvency Standards*.

As with Islamic banking the first *takaful* companies were established prior to any legislation being enacted or special regulations introduced. Salama, the Islamic Arab Insurance Company, was established in Dubai in 1979 as the first modern *takaful* provider. Over the last thirty years its business has grown steadily, both within the UAE, and in Saudi Arabia. Its operations were subsequently extended to Egypt, Senegal, Algeria and Jordan. With a paidup capital of $US 275 million it remains the leading *takaful* provider worldwide,[1] although it is small in relation to the size of the world's leading insurance firms, some of which, such as Allianz, offer *takaful*, in its case from its Bahrain-based operation.[2]

Shari'ah objections to conventional insurance

The Islamic *Fiqh* Academy addressed the issue of the non-acceptability of conventional insurance contracts at a meeting in Jeddah in 1985.[3] They asserted that commercial insurance contracts are inherently uncertain, as the exact circumstances in which pay outs occur are not easily defined. In other words, conventional insurance violates the prohibition of *gharar* as the benefits are dependent on the outcome of future events that are not known at the time the insurance contract is signed.[4] However, this applies to any form of insurance, whether *takaful* or conventional, and if this position is taken there may be a conflict between national laws, requiring for example, car insurance, and *Shari'ah* principles.[5] Fortunately, most *Shari'ah* scholars now interpret *gharar* as applying to legal or contractual uncertainty, not uncertain outcomes.[6] Events, such as a traffic accidents or the death of a policyholder, cannot usually be predicted, but of course risks can be assessed, and insurance premiums based on these assessments. This is the core responsibility of actuaries, whose job is to estimate probabilities of likely outcomes for a group of policyholders. Actuarial work brings social benefits, and is far from being un-Islamic.

The key principle involving the morality of insurance contracts is informed consent. Both parties, the client and the insurance provider, should be aware of the full implications of the contract they are signing. *Gharar* arises where one party, usually the insurance provider, has drafted a contract, with much so called 'small print' burying significant clauses in a mass of information, which the client has difficulty in understanding. In the worst cases this can amount to deliberate deception, or at best the exploitation of a less-informed party, or in other words, the problem of asymmetric information. It should be therefore incumbent on the insurance provider to ensure that the contract is clear and comprehensible, and that the client understands the implications of what they are signing. Insurance regulators, or indeed the *Shari'ah* scholars who advise *takaful* companies, cannot be present for the signing of all, or indeed any contracts, but they have a duty to read the documentation and ensure that there is no legal or contractual uncertainty.[7]

The prohibition of gambling is explicit in the Quran in *Sura* 2: 219 and 5: 93 and believers can be in no doubt about this. Gambling wins are often equated with *maysir*, unearned gains, which are viewed as *haram*, and no *Shari'ah* scholars would seek to justify such gains, although there has been a *fatwa* by Shia scholars that the gain from placing a bet on a horse or camel race may be legitimate if the punter takes great effort to study the form, or past racing history of the runners and the jockeys, as this is time consuming and could be regarded as a type of work. This would not apply to a game of chance however, such as a lottery, as no skill or effort is involved apart from purchasing the ticket.

Should taking out an insurance policy be regarded as analogous to a lottery, with the payment of premium representing a bet on the policyholder being a potential winner? The argument against this is that with insurance the circumstances in which a claim is made, for example, as a result of a vehicle accident, theft of household possessions or damage to a building, involves financial loss, and the purpose of the insurance payout is to simply compensate for this, not to enjoy a windfall gain. Of course policymakers can make fraudulent claims, but that is a matter for the insurance company, and indeed the police and the courts, and should not imply that all general insurance should be prohibited.

Shari'ah scholars have objected specifically to life insurance, the concern being that this constitutes a wager on the policyholder's death, and such matters are in the hands of Allah, not of man. Indeed there is concern over the morality of actuarial work involving the calculation of probability of death, and working out premiums on the basis of this, as the old are likely to be charged more. There may be a reluctance by commercial insurance providers to offer cover to those with a record of poor heath, or if such cover is provided to load the premium, which is regarded as an unfair penalty imposed on the weak and potentially needy.

The other way of looking at the issues is to view life insurance not from the perspective of the policyholder, but rather his or her dependents.[8] This is the concern of providers of family *takaful*, as it is seen as legitimate, indeed highly responsible and desirable, for policyholders to want to protect their families beyond their deaths. Of course, like life insurance, family *takaful* can also be abused, if for example the policyholder fakes an accidental death by committing suicide. Such action would be rather drastic, however, and it is in any case regarded as sinful for Muslims to take their own lives.

Co-operative insurance

There has been extensive debate amongst *Shari'ah* scholars about corporate governance in the insurance industry and whether insurance providers should be organised as commercial companies, with separate shareholders who profit from the premiums paid by the policyholders. Conflicts of interest may arise, as to maximise profits insurance companies may want to minimise costs by restricting claims or paying out less on each claim, but this is against the interests of the policyholders. There is also a basic moral concern that investors in insurance companies are seeking to benefit from the policyholders' fears of potential misfortune, which is viewed as an inappropriate way of making money.

One means of overcoming these problems it to suggest that all insurance providers which are *Shari'ah* compliant should be organised as co-operative institutions.[9] The Islamic *Fiqh* Academy in their 1985 resolution stated that co-operative insurance contracts conform to *Shari'ah* and recommended that such a structure was appropriate for Muslim countries.[10] With such organisations there are no shareholders, rather the policyholders are the owners, and they have an undivided interest in the capital subscribed as long as they continue paying their premiums. The analogy is the membership of a club, where everyone participates. In a co-operative the members aim to pool their resources to help those members in need, with all participants having the assurance that their own needs will be met if necessary, providing there are sufficient funds pooled to finance any payouts. In a co-operative insurance scheme any profits made from investing the premium income are distributed to the policyholders or reinvested to build up reserves, rather than being paid out as dividends to independent shareholders. Here co-operative schemes are equated with mutual organisations, the term used for this type of insurance provision under English Common Law.

The policyholders will not make capital gains, the usual aim of shareholders, as the premiums represent expenditure for a service, the insurance provided, and not an investment.

Investors in an insurance company may, of course, make losses, although if it is a limited-liability company they are only liable for the value of their investment. Policyholders in a co-operative insurance scheme may make no profits if there are substantial payouts, but it would be up to members to decide whether to increase their premiums in the event of a high number of claims. In other words, members of a co-operative organisation do not have unlimited liability, but they may feel a moral duty to increase their premiums if there are a substantial number of genuine claims of increasing cost.

The major limitation of co-operative organisations is that they can only obtain resources from their members and cannot raise equity capital. The members are clients, not equity investors. Although some co-operative insurers in the West have substantial assets, there has been a tendency towards demutualisation in recent years, largely because of a desire to expand the business by becoming a company and offering shares through a stock market. The issuance of equity means the companies can increase resources further by bank borrowings, potentially strengthening their financial position, providing the leverage is kept to acceptable levels.

Those who argued that *takaful* providers should be organised as co-operative institutions rather than profit-making companies seem to have lost the debate, as have those who argued that Islamic finance should be provided through credit unions rather than commercial banks. The same arguments that applied against co-operative organisation for conventional insurance have been used by *takaful* providers, notably the greater flexibility that raising equity capital brings rather than relying on premium income only. There are inconsistencies in this approach, however, as although there is no *Shari'ah* objection to equity investment, the sectors screened out by the Dow Jones Islamic

Indices include insurance. An argument can be made that exclusion does not apply to *takaful* because it is different from conventional insurance, but any difference in how it is organised institutionally appears to have disappeared with the lack of insistence on co-operative status. Furthermore, any leveraging by borrowing immediately raises the question of *riba* or interest, and although under the Dow Jones Islamic Indices criteria companies can leverage for up to one third of their market capitalisation, as will be discussed in Chapter 10, the issue of relying on *riba* financing remains. Of course raising debt capital through other more acceptable instruments such as leasing *ijara* or *istisna'a* project finance would be a possibility, but *takaful* companies do not do this at present.

The organisation of *takaful* with *wakala* contracts and *tabarru* governing premiums

The main distinguishing feature of *takaful* providers is in their contractual documentation. There are two basic forms of contract, one based on the concept of *wakala* (an agency contract) with, in the case of *takaful*, *tabarru* as the distinguishing feature, which can be translated as a donation or offering.[11] The other contract, which will be discussed in the next section, involves a *mudaraba* profit-sharing arrangement. The premium paid under the *tabarru* arrangement is like a membership fee to join a club, which may bring a private benefit to the payee and a social benefit to the other policyholders. It is different to *zakat* payments, which bring a public benefit; rather *tabarru* contributions could be regarded as a type of privatised *zakat*. With *zakat*, as with taxation, the payer does not usually have any discretion over how the revenues are spent, this being a matter for the administrative authorities, who will ultimately be accountable for their decisions to Allah, the remit for the spending being that it should benefit the poor and needy. With *tabarru* on a co-operative basis the payee would have a say on how the premium is used, but if it is offered by a *takaful* company, it is the management that decide. However, there should be clear criteria regarding when benefits are paid that payees should have written into their contracts, and which management should honour. As the payment is dependent on uncertain outcomes, there is an element of *gharar* in *tabarru* arrangements. This is permissible, however, as those paying the *tabarru* contributions are not aiming to profit from the uncertainty, the aim being the pooling of risk: risk management rather than risk taking.

There are, however, significant legal differences between insurance based on conventional contracts and those based on *tabarru*. In particular with the latter a *takaful* operator would not be the owner of the fund, but merely its custodian.[12] The *takaful* operator receives a management fee for their efforts, but any surplus remaining in a *tabarru* fund after all claims have been met belongs to the contributors, not to the management or indeed the shareholders. In theory, it is the policyholders who should be deciding whether any surpluses should be repaid to themselves, used to reduce future premiums, or added to reserves to increase the ability of the *takaful* provider to meet higher future claims. In practice, however, it is the managers who make these decisions, and in the case of a *takaful* company their prime responsibility is to the shareholders as owners, not to the policyholders contributing to the *tabarru* fund. Needless to say there could be conflicts of interest between the shareholders and the policyholders, as building up reserves through the subscriptions of the latter is in the interests of the shareholders, by reducing the potential for losses, while returning surplus funds to the policyholders is

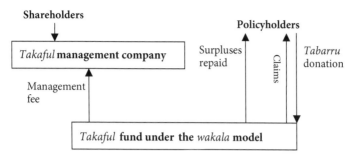

Figure 8.1 *The* wakala *model*

unlikely to be welcomed by the shareholders, even if they are not the actual owners of the *tabarru* fund.

With *wakala* contracts these conflicts of interest are supposed to be addressed by the provisions of the agreement. The *takaful* operators earn a fee, which will usually be around 20 to 35 per cent of the *tabarru* contributions, and therefore the greater the fee income in relation to the operator's costs, the larger the potential dividends for distribution to the shareholders. The flow diagram in Figure 8.1 illustrates the relationship between the different stakeholders, notably the shareholders, the management of the *takaful* company as custodians, and the policyholders contributing to the fund through *tabarru*.

The *tabarru* contributors have a right to any surpluses arising after claims are met; these surpluses do not represent profits, but rather excesses as a result of fortuitous circumstances reducing the value of claims. Similarly, if there is a high level of claims, this may simply reflect unfortunate circumstances such as a hurricane, flood, fire or an increase in mortality because of the spread of infectious disease. In other words, the size of the surplus, or whether there is any, does not reflect management performance, rather the latter is measured by the net profit from fees after expenses have been covered. The aim is to separate the management risks, which are borne by the shareholders, from the insurance risks, which are borne by the policyholders participating in the *takaful* fund through their *tabarru* contributions. This separation can be achieved legally and conceptually, but in practice share prices of listed *takaful* companies are likely to be influenced by news of catastrophes and their impact on payouts. In other words, in financial terms, the determinants of the performance of *takaful* companies may be rather similar to their conventional equivalents.

Takaful contracts based on *mudaraba*

Under the *mudaraba* model the shareholders and policyholders both share in any surpluses generated by the *takaful* fund. The size of the surpluses, or indeed whether there will be a surplus, cannot be known in advance, but the proportionate shares should be stipulated in the contractual agreement. The shares are not necessarily determined by the relative proportions of capital contributed, as the policyholders are not only investors but also purchasers of insurance protection, while the management company could be regarded as the *mudarib*. This corresponds to a traditional *mudaraba* contract where only one of the parties provides the finance, in this case the policyholders, with the other party providing management skills.

The flow diagram in Figure 8.2 illustrates the structure of a *mudaraba* arrangement for providing *takaful*, with the *mudaraba* concept applied to the fund in which the *takaful* company invests and the policyholders pay premiums. The profits are shared between the policyholders and the *takaful* management company according to a predetermined and mutually agreed ratio, although in practice the management company determines the ratio which the policyholder

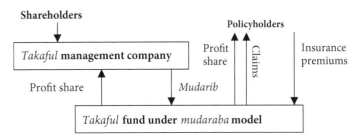

Figure 8.2 *The* mudaraba *model*

either accepts on signing the *takaful* contract or does not accept, and is therefore uninsured. There are some parallels to the with-profits life insurance offered by conventional insurance companies in the case of family *takaful* cover, as although the *takaful* company cannot alter the proportionate shares in the profit once the contracts are signed, they can vary the amount distributed depending on the claims and anticipated claims on the *takaful* fund and the returns on investment by the fund. As with investment *mudaraba* deposits with Islamic banks where there may be a conflict of interest between shareholders and the depositors, a similar conflict can arise with *takaful* between the shareholders looking for dividends and capital gains, and the policyholders seeking a profit share.

The key issue for the policyholders is the transparency of the *takaful* fund and the detail of the financial reporting. The *takaful* management company will need to have its own accounts audited, as this is a regulatory requirement in all jurisdictions. However, the primary purpose of its financial statements is to report to the shareholders, not the policyholders, who have an interest in the *takaful* fund, but not the management company. Conventional with-profits policies are notoriously opaque with regard to the criteria they use in determining with-profit payouts, with

complicated and obscure relationships between the profits declared annually and the terminal bonuses. As *takaful* insurance is supposed to be inherently ethical, *Shari'ah*
scholars serving on the boards of such companies should
insist on a high level of transparency and accountability in
the interests of policyholders, especially with respect to the
takaful fund.

Operational issues

There are a number of operational issues that arise in the
case of *takaful* that do not apply to conventional insurance
companies, not least the need to avoid *riba*. Insurance companies hold a significant proportion of their assets in bonds
or floating-rate notes, which in many respects are well suited
to their needs, as the maturity value is known, the only risk
being of default. Although bonds and notes can be traded,
conventional insurance companies attempt to match the
length to maturity of their assets with their anticipated payments obligations. This cover ensures they are financially
sound, and in recent years, given the increased volatility
of equity markets, both mature and emerging, there has
been a tendency to increase the proportion of bonds and
floating-rate notes to at least 40 per cent of total assets, and
in some cases 50 per cent, and reduce the share of equities
in the total. Equities can ensure capital gains in the long
term, unlike bonds, but with some downturns in equity
markets lasting a decade or more, as in the case of Japan in
the 1990s, and with major Western markets still below their
2001 peaks, there has been a flight to the safety of fixed- and
variable-income securities.

The problem for *takaful* companies is that they cannot
hold conventional bonds or notes as the interest returns
equate to *riba*. The obvious solution is to hold Islamic secu-

rities or *sukuk*, most of which are either *murabaha* based and therefore financially similar to bonds, or *ijara* based with variable returns, the corresponding conventional instrument being a floating-rate note. In Malaysia the substitution of *sukuk* for bonds and notes is not a problem, as there are hundreds available denominated in ringgit, with active trading in *sukuk* for over a decade. The position in the Gulf is very different, with relatively few *sukuk* available until recently, and negligible trading, as those who subscribe to these issues in the first place, usually Islamic banks, hold onto these securities given the absence of other liquid assets available that are *Shari'ah* compliant. A further complication is that many of the *sukuk* in the Gulf are United States dollar denominated rather than being in local currencies in which *takaful* company liabilities are denominated. Although Gulf currencies are pegged to the dollar, there is no guarantee that this peg will remain fixed in the long run, especially if a significant proportion of payments for oil and gas imports cease to be made in dollars, as is likely when the Chinese and Indian currencies become more fully convertible.

Another operational issue is whether conventional insurance companies can offer *takaful*, the parallel being with conventional banks offering *Shari'ah*-compliant products through dedicated windows, counters or branches. The advantage is the huge resources that major insurance companies have and their brand strength that provides assurance to potential clients. This advantage is undermined by the prohibition of any co-mingling of funds within the institution, as if assets that were obtaining a return based on *riba* were present in a *takaful* fund, this would of necessity be *haram*. However, if the *takaful* fund is kept separate from the *takaful* managing company, which could be conventional, this would potentially be acceptable.

The Malaysian *Takaful* Act

Few countries have special laws governing *takaful*, the first specific law being the *Takaful* Act of 1984 (Number 312) of Malaysia.[13] This defined and classified *takaful* business, the major categories being family solidarity business, general *takaful* and re-*takaful*, the latter corresponding to re-insurance or underwriting. Under Section 4 of the Act, *takaful* can only be offered by either companies as defined in the Companies Act of 1965, and therefore subject to its provisions, or societies registered under the Co-operative Societies Act, and thereby subject to its provisions. The purpose of the *Takaful* Act is to provide for a procedure for the registration of *takaful* providers, and to establish the conditions under which they shall operate. Section 6 of the Act is crucial as this stipulates that the operations must conform to *Shari'ah* principles and that the *takaful* operator must establish a *Shari'ah* committee to monitor its activities for compliance. It is the responsibility of the committee to ensure dealings are *halal*, and not the responsibility of those enforcing the Company or Co-operative Societies Acts, nor indeed the *Takaful* Act.

Under Section 15 of the Malaysian *Takaful* Act operators must establish a register of *takaful* certificates, which are the insurance policy documents stating the entitlements of the policyholders. These represent the liabilities of the *takaful* operator, which must be retained for inspection as required. Section 16 of the Act states the conditions governing the *takaful* fund that the operator should establish for family business, in particular that no surpluses should be distributed from the fund without the approval of a qualified actuary, so that the long-term interests of the certificate holders are not undermined by excessive short-term distributions of revenues. Where a fund is wound up the certificate holders have the first claim over any remaining assets. The two other most significant provisions of the Act are Section 17, which deals with the separation of the *takaful* fund from other assets of the operator, and Section 21 that establishes a *takaful* guarantee scheme that is financed by a levy imposed on the *takaful* operators. Funds under this scheme can be used to compensate *takaful* certificate holders in the event of a *takaful* operator becoming insolvent. Happily this has never arisen in over two decades of *takaful* experience in Malaysia, a period in which the average growth of assets managed has been a remarkable 58 per cent per annum.[14] The value of family *takaful* assets exceeds $10 billion, and new contributions have risen to over $400 million annually.[15]

Although having a specific *takaful* law seems appealing and appropriate, other Muslim countries have not followed Malaysia's lead. It can be argued that the provisions of the later Insurance Act of 1996, which covers all insurance companies and not just *takaful* operators, are more significant. The issue is how much value is added by having a *takaful* law, and whether it is simply best to have some references to *takaful* in the existing insurance laws, or indeed tackle the issues at the regulatory level only, if a legal framework is regarded as unnecessary or perhaps needlessly restrictive. In practice, most of the provisions of the *Takaful* Act are concerned with the conditions for registration which are virtually identical to those for conventional companies, and which have been superseded by the 1996 Act. From 2005, Bank Negara, the Central Bank of Malaysia, required *takaful* brokers and loss adjusters to join the same association as their conventional counterparts. As most brokers are involved with both conventional insurance and *takaful*, this provision will not make much difference.[16] Four specialist broker licences have been issued to those dealing exclusively with *takaful* to encourage the industry's development, and four joint *takaful* ventures involving Malaysian and foreign partners have been authorised.

In 2011, very detailed regulatory guidelines were introduced in Malaysia for *takaful* operations,[17] the valuation of *takaful* liabilities[18] and financial reporting by *takaful* operators.[19] The operating guidelines provide for the segregation of the assets of the *takaful* funds from those of the *takaful* operator. For family *takaful*, the protection fund should be separated from the annuity fund with the operators establishing a participants' risk fund and a separate investment fund. This separation also applies to sub funds.

Bahrain's regulatory provision for *takaful*

Bahrain does not have a specific *takaful* law, but the Central Bank of Bahrain, formerly the Monetary Authority, introduced special regulations for *takaful* regulation. These describe the expected characteristics of the *wakala*- and *mudaraba*-based *takaful* operations, and specify that the current practice in Bahrain is to use the *wakala* model for underwriting activities and the *mudaraba* model for the investment activities of *takaful* companies.[20] Some commentators are critical of this so-called mixed model and would like to see a unified set of principles.[21] However, the Central Bank of Bahrain, like Bank Negara, does not specify the rules as to what constitutes a *takaful* product, this being a matter for each firms' *Shari'ah* supervisory board. As in Malaysia, it is obligatory to have such a board. *Takaful* operators must obtain a license to undertake business, but apart from having a *Shari'ah* board, all the other regulations are identical to those for conventional insurance companies operating in Bahrain, including the solvency requirements, record keeping and rules governing matching assets and liabilities to avoid excessive maturity mismatches or currency exposure. The provisions for reporting and financial crime are also the same as for conventional companies, although there is an additional requirement that the policyholders must be informed of the *wakala* and *mudaraba* fees paid to the *takaful* operator.[22] The *wakala* fee should be proportional to the costs associated with establishing and maintaining the contract.

Although much is left to the discretion of the *Shari'ah* boards of the *takaful* operators, and Bahrain can be regarded as an example of a light regulatory environment, the rules are specific where it matters, especially with regard to the disclosure of information to policyholders. In some respects the regulations are more developed than those in Malaysia, despite the latter having a long established *takaful* law. In both jurisdictions the situation is better than in Saudi Arabia, where the long-awaited insurance law passed by royal decree in 2004 was a disappointment from a *takaful* perspective.[23] The law is very general, and contains no reference to *takaful*. There seems to be confusion in the title, as although it is supposed to cover insurance companies 'operating in a co-operative manner' it is not clear what this means, especially as the law refers to joint-stock companies, not co-operative organisations. The regulations issued which accompanied the law are more comprehensive, defining different types of insurance, the conditions for licences being granted, corporate governance and regulatory and supervisory procedures.[24] These seem satisfactory, and in many respects are a sound set of regulations, but again there is no specific reference to *takaful*.

The IFSB guidelines on *takaful*

Detailed guidelines on the governance of *takaful* undertakings and their solvency requirements have been issued by the IFSB in an attempt to highlight international best practice and encourage a degree of standardisation. Rather than each country devising their own rules from first premises, the IFSB guidelines can form the basis for the regulations adopted by its members, and indeed Muslim-minority states such as the United Kingdom which has *takaful* provision.

The guiding principles on governance distinguish between the *mudaraba* and the *wakala* models already discussed.[25] The *takaful* participants as *rabb al maal*, the capital providers, have responsibility for losses, except in the case of negligence or misconduct by the *takaful* operator. The IFSB guidelines also identify a combined model where *wakala* is adopted for underwriting and *mudaraba* for investment activities. The guidelines also define the concept of *tabarru* and the commitments for mutual help involved as well as the related concept of *ta'awun* or mutual assistance.

The provisions on solvency were drafted after the global financial crisis, which had negative implications for *takaful* funds and caused payments difficulties, although no undertaking became insolvent because of timely regulatory intervention. As with the Malaysian regulations much stress is placed on the segregation of funds.[26] There is also provision for *qard*, interest-free loans through transferring assets from the shareholders funds. These should be returned once the liquidity crisis facing the *takaful* undertaking is past. The IFSB recommends that there should be sufficient capital in the shareholders' funds to meet such contingencies arising in the participants risk fund.

It is evident that many of the challenges facing *takaful* undertakings have now been identified and appropriate regulatory provision recommended. There remains however a dearth of regulation in most jurisdictions despite the efforts of the IFSB.

Notes

1. www.salama.ae.
2. www.allianz.com.bh.
3. The Islamic *Fiqh* Academy, Second Session, Resolution Number 9, Jeddah, 22–8 December 1985, p. 1.
4. Mervyn K. Lewis, 'Wealth creation through *takaful*', in Munnawar Iqbal and Rodney Wilson (eds), *Islamic Perspectives on Wealth Creation* (Edinburgh: Edinburgh University Press, 2005), pp. 167–87.
5. Abdullah Al-Fuhaid, 'Car insurance scheme awaits cabinet nod', *Arab News*, Jeddah, 22 June, 2006.
6. Sami Tamer, *The Islamic Financial System* (Frankfurt: Peter Lang European University Studies, 2005), pp. 115–17.
7. Rodney Wilson, 'Concerns and misconceptions in the provision of *takaful*', in Sohail Jaffer (ed.), *Islamic Insurance: Trends, Opportunities and the Future of Takaful* (London: Euromoney Books, 2007), pp. 72–85.
8. Yon Bahiah Wan Aris, *Takaful – an Option to Conventional Insurance: a Malaysian Model*, Staff Paper, Faculty of Business Management, Universiti Teknologi Mara, Selangor, Malaysia, pp. 7–8.
9. Aly Khorshid, *Islamic Insurance: A Modern Approach to Islamic Banking* (London: RoutledgeCurzon, 2004), pp. 97–112.
10. Islamic *Fiqh* Academy, Second Session, Resolution Number 9, Jeddah, 22–28 December, 1985, p. 1, Recommendations 2 and 3.
11. Salahuddin Ahmed, *Islamic Banking, Finance and Insurance: a Global Overview* (Kuala Lumpur: A. S. Noordeen, 2006), p. 515.
12. Abdul Rahim Abdul Wahab, *Takaful Business Models: Wakala Based on Waqf* (Ernst and Young International, 2006), pp. 8–9.
13. Laws of Malaysia, *Takaful* Act 1984, Act 312, Official Gazette, Kuala Lumpur, 31 December 1984.

14. Datuk Zamani Abdul Ghani, 'Building a progressive *takaful* sector in the overall Islamic financial system', keynote address delivered at the Second Seminar on Regulation of *Takaful*, Langkawi, Malaysia, 23 February 2006, p. 2.

15. Bank Negara, *The Takaful Industry Performance*, Kuala Lumpur, 2005.

16. Bank Negara, *Takaful Policies and Developments*, Kuala Lumpur, 2006.

17. Bank Negara, *Guidelines on Takaful Operations Framework*, BNM/RH/GL 004-22, Kuala Lumpur, 2011.

18. Bank Negara, *Guidelines on Valuation Basis for Liabilities of General Takaful Business*, BNM/RH/GL 004-21, Kuala Lumpur, 2011.

19. Bank Negara, *Guidelines on Financial Reporting for Takaful Operators*, BNM/RH/GL 004-6, Kuala Lumpur, 2011.

20. Central Bank of Bahrain Rulebook, *Takaful/Retakaful Module*, Section TA 1.1, Manama, April 2005.

21. Abdul Rahman Tolefat, 'Need for a unified model', *The Takaful Review*, Bahrain Monetary Agency, December 2005, p. 3.

22. Central Bank of Bahrain Rulebook, *Takaful/Retakaful Module*, Section TA 3.1.

23. Law on Supervision of Co-operative Insurance Companies, Royal Decree M/5, Riyadh, 1/5/1420 H.

24. Saudi Arabian Monetary Agency, *Insurance Regulations*, Riyadh, 2005.

25. IFSB, *Guiding Principles on Governance for Takaful (Islamic Insurance) Undertakings*, Kuala Lumpur, December 2009, p. 4.

26. IFSB, *Standard on Solvency Requirements for Takaful (Islamic Insurance) Undertakings*, Kuala Lumpur, December 2011, p. 3.

CHAPTER 9
SUKUK STRUCTURES AND THEIR CONTRACTUAL IMPLICATIONS

Sukuk, sometimes referred to as Islamic bonds, are better described as Islamic investment certificates. This distinction is crucial, as *sukuk* should not merely be regarded as a substitute for conventional interest-based securities. The aim is not simply to engineer financial products that mimic fixed-rate bills and bonds and floating-rate notes as understood in the West, but rather to develop innovative types of assets that comply with *Shari'ah* Islamic law. This means firstly, transparency and clarity of rights and obligations; secondly, that income from the securities must be related to the purpose for which the funding is used; and thirdly, that the securities should be backed by real underlying assets rather than being simply paper derivatives.

Islamic fixed-income securities are already emerging as a significant class of asset, as potentially important for the Muslim investor as conventional bonds are for investors more generally. In addition for non-Muslims, who already own conventional bonds, the acquisition of *sukuks* introduces a new asset class into their portfolios, bringing further welcome diversity and possibly reducing risk.

The legitimacy of *sukuk*

Although there is no compulsion to comply with the rulings of the *Fiqh* Academy of the Organisation of the Islamic Conference, their rulings carry considerable weight with most Islamic financial institutions and their *Shari'ah* committees and advisors. At the request of delegates from Jordan, Pakistan and Malaysia the *Fiqh* Academy considered the question of Islamic investment certificates at their fourth annual plenary session held in Jeddah in February 1988. They noted that *Shari'ah* encourages the documentation of contracts as stipulated in *Sura* 2: 282 of the Quran:

> When ye deal with each other, in transactions involving future obligations in a fixed period of time, reduce them to writing . . . It is more just in the sight of God, more suitable as evidence and more convenient to prevent doubts among yourselves.[1]

Subject to proper legal documentation the *Fiqh* Academy, under decision number 5 of 1988, ruled firstly, that any collection of assets can be represented in a written note or bond, and secondly, that this bond or note can be sold at a market price provided that the composition of the group of assets, represented by the security, consists of a majority of physical assets and financial rights, with only a minority being cash and interpersonal debts.[2]

Why have Islamic bonds?

Conventional bonds that yield interest or *riba* are of course prohibited under *Shari'ah* law. Furthermore, those who buy and sell conventional bonds are rarely interested in what is actually being financed through the bond issue, which could include activities and industries that are deemed *haram*, such as the production or sale of alcohol. Companies that are highly leveraged with bank debt may seek refinancing through issuing bonds, but such companies are not regarded as suitable for Muslim investors.

The aim of bond traders is usually to make capital gains, as fixed-interest bond prices increase when variable market interest rates fall. Bond trading is therefore largely about exploiting interest rate developments, and of trading in paper that is usually unrelated to the value of any underlying asset. The major risk for holders of conventional bonds is of payments default, but this risk is usually assessed solely on the basis of credit ratings, with the ratings agency rather than the bond purchaser estimating the risk. Hence, the bonds are regarded as mere pieces of paper with third parties estimating the risk and the purchaser only at best making a risk/return calculation without any reference to the business being financed.

Shari'ah scholars, most notably Muhammad Taqi Usmani, have stressed that one of the distinguishing features legitimising Islamic finance is that it must involve the funding of trade in, or the production of, real assets.[3] Merely funding the purchase of financial securities would involve second-order financing, akin to lending for derivative purchases, the subsequent gearing being speculative and increasing uncertainty or *gharar*. Hence, with *murabaha*, commodities are purchased on behalf of a client and resold to the client, the temporary ownership of the commodity justifying the financier's markup. *Istisna* involves the financing of manufacturing capacity through pre-production payments, but these relate to construction or equipment purchases, where real capacity can be identified. Similarly, *ijara* involves the leasing of real assets, the use of the assets justifying the payment of rental to the owner.

As Islamic finance is by nature participatory, purchasers of *sukuk* securities have arguably the right to information on the purposes for which their monies are to be allocated. In other words, the funding raised through Islamic bond issues should be hypothecated or earmarked rather than used for general unspecified purposes, whether by a sovereign or corporate issuer. This implies that identifiable assets should back Islamic bonds.

Sukuk structures

As with conventional debt securities *sukuk* are issued for a fixed time period rather than in perpetuity as in the case of equity. The time period can vary from three months in the case of *sukuk* that are similar to treasury bills, to five or even ten years for those that resemble conventional notes. Most *sukuk* are either *murabaha* or *ijara* based, with the former offering a fixed return like a bond, while the latter provides a variable return similar to a floating-rate note.[4]

What makes a *sukuk* acceptable under *Shari'ah* law is that it must be backed by a real asset such as a piece of land, a building or an item of equipment, and therefore when *sukuk* are bought and sold the purchaser and seller are dealing indirectly in a real asset, and not simply trading paper. With a *murabaha sukuk* an Islamic bank securitises its trading transactions with a proportion of the fixed markup providing the return to the *sukuk* investor, and the bank using the repayment from its trading client to repay the *sukuk* holder on termination of the contract. In this case the bank originates the *sukuk* on its own behalf, but more often it acts as arranger for a trading company that seeks to originate a *murabaha sukuk* to raise funds to cover its purchase of a commodity. In this case the commodity acquired serves as the asset backing the *sukuk*.

Salam sukuk

In practice *salam* (or *bay' al salam*) structures have proved more popular for short-run financing *sukuk* than *murabaha* as the latter usually involves commodity trading, the finance of which is not the aim of most *sukuk* issues. *Salam* simply refers to a sale in which payment is made in advance by the buyer, and the delivery of the asset is deferred by the seller. The period involved is usually short, as with *murabaha*, three months being typical. In practice a *salam sukuk* can be considered as a *Shari'ah*-compliant substitute for a conventional treasury bill issued for three-months short-term financing by governments, as the return and the period to maturity are fixed when the offer is made. Such *salam sukuk* have been issued by the Central Bank of Bahrain at three-monthly intervals since 2002 as part of the short-term financing facilities arranged on behalf of the government of Bahrain.[5]

A typical *salam sukuk* structure is shown in Figure 9.1, with the issuer a special purpose vehicle (SPV) created as a legal entity for the duration of the *sukuk* with the sole purpose of administrating the payments made to the investors and holding the title to the assets on which the *sukuk* is based.[6] The SPV can be regarded as a non-profit-making trust, indeed the trust structures for which there are special provision in English law are widely used for cross-border *sukuk* issues. As Malaysian law is very similar to English law, with comparable provision for trusts, this has facilitated the development of a market in *sukuk* in Kuala Lumpur.

The first stage in the operation of a *sukuk* is when the originator (for example, the government of Bahrain) transfers a title to the assets to the SPV, which in turn issues certificates of participation to the investors, who may be Islamic banks,

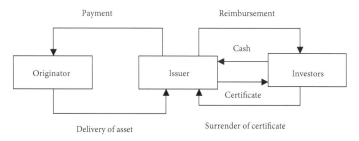

Figure 9.1 Salam sukuk *structure*

takaful Islamic insurance companies or investment companies that want to hold their liquid assets in a *Shariʻah*-
compliant form. The certificates of participation represent
an undivided right to an interest in the assets, which means
that the assets cannot be sold to another party for the duration of the *sukuk*. In return for the certificates of participation the investors make an up-front payment which entitles
the investor to a future refund of the investment plus a fixed
markup agreed in advance. It is because the initial payment
is in advance, or up front, that designates the structure as
salam.

As the diagram shows, the initial cash provided by the
investors and collected by the SPV is used to make a payment to the originator in return for an undertaking to
deliver the asset at maturity. At that stage, typically after
three months, the SPV takes delivery of the asset, but sells
it back to the originator. The proceeds from this sale are
then used to reimburse the cash provided by the Islamic
investors, and provide them with the pre-agreed markup
return in relation to their investment. Before obtaining
the return of their cash and the markup the investors have
to surrender their certificates of participation to the SPV,
implying they have no further right to an interest in the
assets.

Ijara sukuk

Under an *ijara* contract the usufruct of a particular property is transferred from the owner to another person in exchange for a rental payment. It is in other words a leasing agreement, with the owner, referred to as the *mujir* and the lessee called the *mustajir*. The rent paid to the owner is called *ujrah*. *Shari'ah* law imposes restrictions on *ijara* agreements that are not present in conventional leasing contracts, largely to protect the parties as far as possible from uncertainty and to ensure there is no ambiguity in the agreement.

With an *ijara sukuk* the prime function of the SPV throughout its life is the management of the *sukuk*, in particular the receipt of rent from the client for the leased asset and the payment to *sukuk* investors.[7] When the *sukuk* matures the SPV no longer has a role, and consequently it is wound up and ceases to exist as a legal entity. With this arrangement the SPV has no other obligations apart from those involved with the specific *sukuk*, and therefore it has none of the risks associated with a bank, nor is it subject to bank regulation. In other words, the SPV is bankruptcy remote, and hence is attractive to both the issuers and the investors. This is seen as a major advantage, justifying the relatively high legal costs of establishing the SPV. The risk assessment of the *sukuk* will simply depend on the client's perceived ability to make the payments to the SPV, which in the case of a government is the sovereign risk, and in the case of a company is the corporate risk. Not surprisingly this simple *ijara* SPV structure accounts for the overwhelming majority of *sukuk* issued to date.

As an *ijara* contract is for a predetermined period, and as the rent provides a regular monthly, quarterly or annual income, it is clearly well suited to be covered by the issue of securities that have many of the characteristics of bonds. As *ijara* bonds are securities representing the ownership of well-defined assets subject to a lease contract they may be traded in a secondary market at the prevailing price determined by market forces. There are many originators of *ijara* securities including Ministries of Finance, Central Banks, municipalities, authorities responsible for *waqf* or religious endowments, investment banks or public or private companies. Such securities have maturity periods of three years or more, although at present there are few issues running for more than ten years.

It is important to note that *ijara* certificates or securities represent a proportionate ownership claim over a leased asset, and therefore those who hold the securities have ownership responsibilities that only terminate when the securities mature or if they are sold to another party, who then assumes the responsibilities.[8] In practice it is the SPV which exercises the ownership responsibilities on behalf of the investors. Unlike shareholders in the equity of a joint-stock company, whose ownership rights are in perpetuity, those of the holder of an *ijara* certificate are for a fixed period. Furthermore, holders of *ijara* certificates only benefit from the monthly, quarterly or annual rental payments, as they cannot enjoy capital gains that are usually the main motivation for equity investments. On the other hand, investment in *ijara* certificates is less risky than equities, and the income stream is for a predetermined regular amount, usually benchmarked to an agreed indicator, whereas any dividends accruing to equity investors can be subject to considerable variation.

The diagram below illustrating an *ijara sukuk* structure is similar to that for a *salam sukuk*, but variable rental payments are made rather than the markup being fixed. As with the *salam sukuk* the Islamic investors put in cash in return

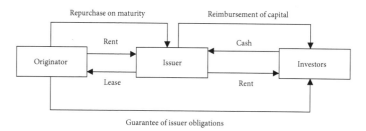

Figure 9.2 Ijara sukuk *structure*

for certificates of participation which gives them an undivided interest in the underlying asset. As the duration of the financing is much longer, usually at least five years, the title to the asset is held by the SPV, not the originator, as the cash provided by the investors is used by the SPV to acquire the title from the originator. It is the sale of the title that provides the originator with the financing. As the originator will continue to use the asset after it is sold there is a leaseback arrangement where the originator pays rent to the SPV for the usufruct rights. It is these payments that enable the SPV to pay the investors a stream of rental payments representing the coupon on the *sukuk* security.

As *ijara sukuk* are typically issued for periods of at least five years it is usual for the investors to receive a direct guarantee from the originator. This provides assurance to the investors given that the ability of the SPV to fulfil its commitments ultimately depends on the rental payments made by the originator. This guarantee also includes the obligation by the originator to buy back the asset at the end of the period of the lease for an amount that is equivalent to the original price at which the asset was sold. There can, in other words, be no capital gain or loss for the SPV or the originator. It is the buy-back by the issuer that provides the funds for the reimbursement of the investors of the sum they originally invested, also without capital gains or losses. The rating of the *ijara sukuk* depends on the rating agency's evaluation of the ability of the originator to honour these commitments, and if the financial circumstances of the originator change during the leasing period this may result in a downward or upward adjustment in the rating.[9]

Musharaka sukuk

As the majority of *sukuk* are *ijara* based this structure is well tried and tested, which reduces the legal costs and structuring fees involved with new issues. There is nevertheless an interest in innovation in *sukuk* by both issuers and law firms, partly because of the prestige involved in being first in the field with a new innovative product, but also more fundamentally because partnership structures based on *musharaka* are much closer to the traditional forms of business organisation and financing long practiced informally in the Muslim world.[10] In the case of *istisna'a* structures, another possible innovative *sukuk*, their credibility comes from the practical consideration of them being well suited for project finance, which is increasingly important in Muslim states where governments are more and more reluctant to simply fund new infrastructure schemes from their own budgets, and there is a greater stress on private-public partnerships.

It is the diminishing *musharaka* structure that has the most potential for *sukuk* as this involves an Islamic bank or *Shari'ah*-compliant investment company providing upfront investment funding to the originator, with both parties establishing an SPV to administer the *sukuk*. The financial structure is similar to an *ijara sukuk*, but the payments flows are quite distinct, both legally and operationally. The originator sells an asset to the SPV while entering a partnership rather than a leasing agreement. The Islamic investors pay out cash as before, but receive certificates of partnership rather than simply certificates of participation. The legal implication is that both the investors and the originator are partners in the SPV but that the share of the investors in the SPV will diminish over time as instalment payments are made by the originator to repurchase the asset. It is these repayments, plus the rental paid by the originator for the use of the asset, that provides the income stream for the investors. Whereas with a *salam, ijara* or *musharaka sukuk* the investors receive the return of their capital at the end of the period, with a diminishing *musharaka* structure they receive the return of their capital in instalments, with the final instalment terminating the partnership.

There is considerable flexibility with diminishing *musharaka sukuk* with respect to the payments schedule and amounts, as long as the parties agree on the terms when the partnership involving the SPV is established. The repayments will usually be monthly or quarterly, but they do not have to be in equal instalments. Smaller instalments could be made during the initial period of the *sukuk*, with most of the asset value or SPV capital remaining with the investors, but the amount of the instalment payments could increase in an exponential or logarithmic fashion according to some predetermined formula. As the originator increases their share of the asset through the buy-back they might be expected to pay less rent for the remaining share, but this does not necessarily have to be the case, especially if there is capital appreciation in the value of the asset. In other words, when instalment and rental payments are aggregated, they might be constant, diminishing or increasing over time, provided both parties agree to the formula used and the documentation is transparent.

Mudaraba tradable certificates

It should be noted that holders of *mudaraba* notes do not enjoy the same rights and benefits as equity investors, as they are only entitled to a profit share and there is no provision for capital gains based on the market valuation of the company. The *mudaraba*-note holders are not registered owners, and cannot attend or vote at the annual general meeting. On the other hand although the value of their notes cannot be guaranteed, it is the shareholders rather than *mudaraba*-note holders who are more likely to suffer from capital losses in the event of the company performing badly, and in the case of bankruptcy the note holders will be in a higher position in the pecking order to equity investors who are likely to lose all of their money.

Mudaraba certificates were first issued in Pakistan under an ordinance passed in 1980 with companies with a paid-up capital of at least 5 million rupees allowed to offer such certificates to the public.[11] These enjoyed limited success, but the returns were disappointing, partly reflecting the weakness of the companies involved and the poor performance more generally of Pakistan's economy. The Jordanian Ministry of *Waqf* has issued *mudaraba* bonds, although there was some controversy concerning the guarantee of capital on maturity, and the Islamic *Fiqh* Academy recommended that this should be a voluntary commitment, referred to as *tabarru*, rather than an absolute guarantee. Conventional banks in Egypt, notably Bank Misr, have also issued *mudaraba* certificates as one of their Islamic products, but there has been some concern about possible co-mingling of funds and the guarantees of the bond principal, which violates the *Shari'ah* principle of no reward without risk or effort.[12]

Istisna'a bonds

Project financing can be undertaken through an *istisna'a* contract whereby funds are advanced to pay for the supplies and labour costs by an Islamic bank. Once the project is completed the advances are repaid from the revenue derived from the project. Originally *istisna'a* was seen as an appropriate way of financing manufacturing, as goods have to be produced and costs incurred before they are sold.

To introduce bonds based on *istisna'a*, a parallel *istisna'a* contract is generally used, whereby the financier enters a contract with a subcontractor who actually builds the facility being financed. To use *istisna'a* the public authority or private company commissioning the project provides details of the specifications and timing of the schemes. The financier then sets these out in the tender documents. Bids are subsequently invited from contractors who will specify how then intend to sell completed parts of the project over time and the amount of each payments instalment expected. These instalments will include an element of profit over the construction costs. As the financier is expecting a stream of payments over a specified period certificates can be issued based on the income expected.

It should be noted that as the deferred price certificates represent debt obligations they cannot be traded for cash at below face value in a secondary market. They can however be used to purchase goods or services whose price is equal to the face value of the certificate. The purchase price of the goods may be less than the deferred price as this represents a trading transaction. Permission to transfer the debt contract from the financier to a supplier of goods and services must be sought from the original debtor, the public authority or private company commissioning the project.[13]

Sukuk pricing and risk assessment

The major criticism of *ijara sukuk* is that the return is usually benchmarked to the London Inter-bank Offer Rate (LIBOR) on $US dollar funds or the equivalent local rate in the case of issues in Malaysian ringgit, UAE dirham or Saudi riyal. This is of course an interest rate, and although it is only used for pricing, and the payments associated with the *ijara* can be regarded as rents, the close link of the interest-based pricing with *riba* worries many *Shari'ah* scholars.

The problem for the financiers is that they want the investors to regard the *sukuk* as identical to their equivalent conventional asset classes rather than being distinctive from a financial perspective, as this simplifies risk assessment. Investors are more relaxed if a security has a familiar structure rather than being unknown and untried. Hence the innovation with *sukuk* is solely legal; their distinctive characteristic being *Shari'ah* compliance, but there has been no financial innovation.

Risk-rating agencies are willing to rate *sukuk* because of their familiar structures, with assurance for investors provided by Standard and Poor's, the global leader, or Capital Intelligence, the agency that specialises in rating Middle Eastern banks. A dedicated Islamic *sukuk* rating agency has been established by the Islamic Development Bank, and the Rating Agency of Malaysia has acquired much experience of *sukuk* evaluation, but these use similar criteria to other rating institutions.

Financial innovation with *sukuk*

For *sukuk* to be distinctive from conventional securities financial engineering will be necessary to bring about new types of products. These may be initially more costly for the clients in terms of the rates that are offered to attract investors, and the latter may be uncertain and cautious about committing their funds to the unfamiliar. Conventional and Islamic banks involved with new types of *sukuk* will incur product-development costs, often without the certainty that they can be recouped. Yet for those who do launch successful products the rewards could ultimately be high, as even if other institutions copy the same formula, the recognition that comes from being first in the field can be very helpful for longer-term business generation.

The key to innovation is to focus on pricing and risk characteristics. For sovereign *sukuk*, pricing could be based on real macroeconomic variables such as GDP growth rather than interest benchmarks. When GDP growth was high government tax revenue would usually increase more rapidly, especially for countries with income or sales taxes. This would enable governments to pay a higher return to investors in their sovereign *sukuk*. Conversely, when GDP growth was lower, government revenue would be lower, implying a reduced capacity to service debt and pay *sukuk* holders. In other words, *sukuk* holders would be taking on some of the sovereign risk.[14] By sharing risk with governments and reducing their obligations in times of difficulty, the risk of default would be reduced. This might enable sovereign *sukuk* based on GDP benchmarks to be more favourably rated than the present 'conventional' *sukuk*.

The IFSB and AAOIFI guidelines on *sukuk*

As in other areas of Islamic finance it is the IFSB that has issued guidelines on *sukuk* which have become de facto the recognised standards.[15] These draw on the experiences of over a decade of active *sukuk* issuance and trading and the issues raised by *Shari'ah* scholars as well as *sukuk* originators and investors and the law firms representing their interests. Asset-based *sukuk*, where there is a binding promise by the originator to re-purchase the asset on maturity, are distinguished from pass-through *sukuk*. With the latter it is the SPV as issuer which gives the investor recourse to the assets in the event of a default by the originator. *Shari'ah*-compliant credit enhancement may be sought, which will typically be provided by the arranger, an investment bank, for a fee. The aim is to ensure that the investor has their funds returned at par value and are not exposed to default or market risk, the latter arising through the impairment of the assets or a fall in their market value.

Such undertakings potentially undermine the *Shari'ah* principle of risk sharing which is inherent in Islamic financial contracts. Muhammad Taqi Usmani, the Chairman of the AAOIFI *Shari'ah* Board was especially critical at a conference in Bahrain in 2007, declaring that most *sukuk* were not *Shari'ah* compliant. Subsequently AAOIFI issued clarification indicating that Usmani's criticisms applied to *sukuk* based on *musharaka* and *mudaraba* where investors were liable to market risk, but not to *salam*, *ijara* and *istisna'a sukuk*, where the risk was that of default.[16]

The first AAOIFI principle was that *sukuk* holdings should represent real ownership of assets. Second, there should be no conventional debt liabilities with the revenue stream from such debts representing part, or all, of the revenue stream to the *sukuk* investors. *Sukuk* investments are not creditor-debtor contracts as under *Shari'ah* debt receipts cannot be traded. Third, loans cannot be provided to *sukuk* investors when revenues are below those expected, although reserves can be set aside for such compensation provided this is stipulated in the *sukuk* contracts. Fourth, the market value of the asset or firm being funded should determine the amount repaid to the investors on the maturity of a *mudaraba* or *musharaka sukuk*. The assumption is that market risk is inherent in partnership contracts and should not be borne solely by the party being financed. Provision five states that in the case of *ijara sukuk*, however, it is permissible to repay an amount equivalent to the nominal value of the original investment as these are not partnership contracts. A consequence of this ruling was that *ijara* structures became even more widely used after 2008 and there was no new issuance of *mudaraba* or *musharaka* as investors were reluctant to be exposed to market risk.

Sukuk are primarily institutional investment vehicles rather than being promoted for retail investors. The latter can however gain exposure to *sukuk* through an Islamic collective scheme, or in other words, a *Shari'ah*-compliant managed fund. The contractual relations governing such funds and their operations are dealt with in the next chapter.

Notes

1. *The Holy Koran*, text, translation and commentary by Abdullah Yusuf Ali (Kuwait: That Es-Salasil Printing and Publishing, [1934] reprint 1988).

2. Monzer Kahf, 'The use of *ijara* bonds for bridging the budget gap', in Ausaf Ahmad and Tariqullah Khan (eds), *Islamic Financial Instruments for Public Resource Mobilisation*, Islamic Research and Training Institute, Islamic Development Bank, Seminar Proceedings Number 39, Jeddah, 1997, p. 293.

3. Muhammad Taqi Usmani, *An Introduction to Islamic Finance* (The Hague: Kluwer Law International, 2002), pp. xiv–xvii.

4. Bilal Aquil, 'Tracking the progress of *sukuk*', *Islamic Banking and Finance Magazine*, Dubai, 14 October 2005.

5. Bahrain Monetary Agency, *Islamic Banking and Finance in the Kingdom of Bahrain* (Manama: Bahrain Monetary Agency, 2002), pp. 72–5.

6. Adrian Dommisse and Wasif Kazi, 'Securitisation and *shariah* law', *Middle East Banker*, Dubai, 1 July 2005.

7. Aseambankers, *Capitalising on Opportunities in the Sukuk Industry* (Kuala Lumpur: Aseambankers, 2005), pp. 1–5.

8. Muhammad Taqi Usmani, *An Introduction to Islamic Finance* (The Hague: Kluwer Law International, 2002), pp. 80–1.

9. Kristel Richard (Standard and Poor's), 'A closer look at *ijara sukuk*', *Banker Middle East*, Dubai, March 2005, pp. 1–5.

10. Muhammad Nejatullah Siddiqi, *Partnership and Profit Sharing in Islamic Law* (Leicester: The Islamic Foundation, 1985), pp. 9–18.

11. Christine Gieraths, 'Pakistan: main participants and financial products of the Islamisation process', in Rodney Wilson (ed.), *Islamic Financial Markets* (London: Routledge, 1990), pp. 171–95.

12. Abul Rahman Yousri Ahmed, 'Islamic securities in Muslim country's stock markets and an assessment of the need for an Islamic secondary market', *International Journal of Islamic Financial Services*, 3: 1, 1995.

13. Muhammad al-Bashir Muhammad al-Amine, 'The Islamic bonds market: possibilities and challenges', *International Journal of Islamic Financial Services*, 3: 1, 1995.

14. Ali Arsalan Tariq, 'Managing financial risks of *sukuk* structures', MSc Dissertation, Loughborough University, September 2004, pp. 43–54.

15. IFSB, *Capital Adequacy Requirements for Sukuk Securitisations and Real Estate Investment*, Kuala Lumpur, January 2009.

16. AAOIFI, *Sukuk Statement*, Bahrain, 2008, pp. 1–3.

CHAPTER 10

SHARI'AH MONITORING AND REGULATORY SUPERVISION OF ISLAMIC FUNDS

There are close parallels between the Islamic fund management industry and the principles of ethical fund management, notably with respect to the criteria for stock selection for inclusion in a portfolio, or screening as it is more commonly called. Although both Islamic and ethical funds can include bonds and even assets such as real estate, most of the investment has been in traded equities. The focus of this chapter is on how to screen equity investments in stock markets throughout the world to identify companies that are potentially acceptable to Islamic investors in terms of their degree of compliance with *Shari'ah* law.

Principles and practices of Islamic equity investment

Before examining the specific criteria used in screening, it is important to be aware of the key principles guiding Islamic equity investment. These include the legitimacy of investing in stock markets given the inherent uncertainty over equity prices, concern over *gharar* or ambiguity in the information provided to investors, worries about the immorality of speculative activity and awareness of the temptation to get involved in *haram* activities such as insider dealing, where those involved in buying and selling shares try to profit from information denied to other investors.[1] This could include fund managers using their client's money to create opportunities for personal profit by buying into and selling from their own funds.[2]

Clearly there are potential conflicts of interest and moral hazard problems involved in Islamic equity investment that highlight the need for transparency and proper monitoring and regulation of the industry. There will always be risk and uncertainty with equity investment, but managers of Islamic funds have a moral as well as a legal obligation to ensure that the investor has clear information about how the investments are being deployed.

Islamic fund managers have less autonomy than conventional fund managers, as they are usually accountable to a *Shari'ah* committee or *Shari'ah* advisor who rules on the screening criteria for stock selection and how this is to be interpreted under changing market conditions and company circumstances. In practice, not all funds have their own *Shari'ah* committee, but rather rely on the screening criteria adopted by the international institutions such as the Dow Jones Islamic Indexes, and approved by the Dow Jones *Shari'ah* board, although this should not be seen as a substitute for local *Shari'ah* monitoring.

This has been a helpful development, as it means that an international panel of well-known and respected *Shari'ah* scholars is addressing screening decisions. These include Sheikh Abdul Sattar Abu Ghuddah of Syria, Sheikh Justice Muhammad Taqi Usmani of Pakistan, Sheikh Nizam Yaquby of Bahrain, Skeikh Mohammed Elgari of Saudi Arabia, Sheikh Yusuf Talal DeLorenzo of the United States and Sheikh Mohd Daud Baker of Malaysia.[3] This international representation has helped encourage standardisation of screening criteria and increased the confidence of Muslim investors that their investments are being monitored in a competent manner that complies with *Shari'ah* law.

Most of the companies that Islamic equity funds invest in are quoted on Western markets, largely because these are the predominant centres for stock-market activity, the only markets in the Muslim world with a market capitalisation exceeding $100 billion being Saudi Arabia, Turkey, Indonesia and Malaysia. Islamic fund management involves the harnessing and recycling of Muslim funds into the global economy, rather than confining them to the Muslim world where risks are often higher reflecting more volatile stock prices. It is about ensuring that Muslim investors are not over-exposed to risk and hence disadvantaged.

There is no prohibition under *Shari'ah* law in investing in a listed company run by non-Muslims in a predominately non-Muslim country. This is not an ideal situation from an Islamic perspective, but it is recognised that a degree of compromise and pragmatism is necessary, even if the approach arguably represents an acceptable second-best solution in a global financial scene dominated by *riba*-based finance.

Differences between equity investment and *musharaka* and *mudaraba*

For Muslims, equity investment is certainly preferable to placing funds in interest-yielding bonds or certificates of deposit, even if equities themselves cannot be equated with Islamic financial instruments such as *mudaraba* or *musharaka* partnership contracts. Equities can be disposed of at any time without the permission of the company being financed, unlike *mudaraba* and *musharaka* investments that are for a fixed time period agreed between the financier, as *rab al maal*, and the manager or entrepreneur as *mudarib*. The potential liquidity is of course one of the most attractive features of equities, whereas *mudaraba* and *musharaka* investments are inherently illiquid, although the former can be progressively retired if there is a diminishing *mudaraba* contract.

Furthermore, equity investors can sell some of their shares in a particular company, whereas a single *mudaraba* or *musharaka* is indivisible. *Musharaka* is really more like venture capital and hence much more risky than equity investment in listed stock. In the case of *mudaraba* there is little risk for the holder of an investment deposit on such terms with an Islamic bank, but there is more risk in the second tier of a *mudaraba* involving the bank as an investor in a business.

The investor in a *mudaraba* and *musharaka* contract enjoys the possibility of a share in the profits of the business, but not the capital gains. In contrast, most investors in equities and equity-based funds hope for capital gains, and even investors in income funds will hope that the value of their assets keeps pace with inflation unlike the principal in a bank or building society. For these reasons equity investments have to be regarded as occupying a different place in a portfolio to *mudaraba* and *musharaka* investments, but a place which Islamic investors have the right to occupy according to the *Fiqh* Academy ruling of 1996, unlike *riba*-based investments in conventional bonds or similar instruments which are strictly *haram*.

The corporate governance systems involving *mudaraba* and *musharaka* are quite different to those for listed companies. *Mudaraba* and *musharaka* involve partnership arrangements, with agreement required from all parties before new capital is raised or funds are withdrawn.[4]

In contrast with listed companies the shareholders do not enjoy a right of veto, but rather financing decisions can be ratified by a simple majority of those owning more than 50 per cent of the company. In practice, small groups of pro-active shareholders, perhaps with a moral agenda, can exercise much influence over company policy even if they do not own a majority of the shares. There is consequently much greater flexibility and fluidity than with traditional partnerships.

The advantages of fund management for Islamic equity investments

Muslims like any other investors can of course purchase equities directly and build up their own investment port-folios rather than investing indirectly through fund management groups and incurring management charges. The search costs are, however, higher for Muslim direct-equity investors if they want to satisfy themselves that the companies they are investing in are acceptable from the point of view of *Shari'ah* law. Screening requires a considerable amount of information which can only be ascertained by scrutinising the company's annual reports and accounts, perhaps over a period of several years to discern trends, and discover the extent to which the company has kept to its stated intentions. Skills are also needed to know what figures to use to calculate ratios which are important from an Islamic perspective, notably leverage, the ratio of debt to equity.

Those with large amounts to invest can of course engage their own personal independent financial consultants, accountants, and even *Shari'ah* advisors, but the problems of interpreting and co-ordinating potentially conflicting advice are far from easy. Islamic banks are not geared up to providing such an integrated portfolio management service for their more wealthy clients, the favoured alternative being to suggest that the client opens a restricted investment account in which the depositor shares in profits of the businesses using his funds rather than the banks profits, as is usually the case with investment accounts. Restricted investment accounts approximate closely to a one-way multiple *mudaraba* with the bank charging a management fee as intermediary and the client having a direct (one-way) relationship with the companies (hence multiple *mudaraba*) being financed.[5] This is not a substitute for an equity portfolio, however, as the specified investment is for a fixed time period, and returns are based on profit sharing, not capital gains.

If there were specialist firms of stockbrokers providing dedicated Islamic portfolio management services on behalf of Muslim investors this would be an acceptable alternative to the use of fund management services, but such services have yet to emerge although Islamic asset-management groups such as Al Rajhi Bank of Saudi Arabia, AmInvestment Bank of Malaysia and Bank of London and the Middle East offer partial services of this type. They are not, however, stockbroking companies or equity specialists.

For most Muslim investors the most sensible route into equity markets is through fund-management groups that offer Islamic services. There are four basic advantages for the Muslim investor from using such services:

1. a broader portfolio diversification which can reduce risk for a given return or increase return for a given risk;
2. the ability to participate in new risks, including unquoted companies whose shares are not available on the open market;
3. professional portfolio management by fund managers

who are usually better informed and qualified to make investment decisions than individual investors;

4. smaller transaction costs as the fund manager can buy and sell stock in large amounts.

Sector screens for *Shariʿah* compliance

To ensure that the companies selected for the investment are acceptable from the perspective of *Shariʿah* law, a fund-management group can screen the prospective companies to be included in the portfolio. As with ethical investment selection, both positive and negative criteria can be used. Negative criteria involve excluding companies whose major purpose is the production or distribution of alcohol or pork products or the management of gambling facilities. Investment in conventional *riba*-based financial institutions may also be regarded as *haram*. Some investors may be concerned with political criteria, viewing companies involved in Israel as threatening the legitimate interests of Muslims in Jerusalem. On the other hand, companies that are promoting trade with Muslim countries may be viewed positively, as will companies involved in the economies of the Islamic world through their investments.

There are three major index specialists who provide Islamic screening: the S&P Global Benchmark *Shariʿah* Index Series, the Financial Times FTSE Global Islamic Index Series and the Dow Jones Islamic Indexes. The sectors specifically excluded from all three indexes include those involved with alcohol, tobacco, gaming, pork production and distribution and conventional banking and insurance.[6] There is also a general screen excluding activities deemed offensive to the principles of Islam. Companies that are not primarily involved with *haram* activities, but where such activities nevertheless constitute a significant proportion of their business are also excluded. This exact proportion is not however specified, as there is no reference in Quranic teaching to percentages. Rather the implication is that each company should be examined on its own merits. Companies that are classified as being in acceptable industry groups may also be excluded if they have a significant ownership stake in, or derive revenue from, *haram* activities.

Some investors may prefer to avoid investing in airlines, hotels or supermarket chains that serve and sell alcohol, even though this is a minor part of their business. This would, however, result in a much more restricted potential portfolio selection. Usually businesses are defined by their prime activity, which makes a hotel group or airline acceptable, but a brewery unacceptable. There are parallels with ethical-investment funds that avoid investing in tobacco companies, but may invest in retail groups selling cigarettes alongside other items.

The *Shari'ah* Advisory Council (SAC) of the Securities Exchange Commission of Malaysia has drawn up detailed criteria for screening companies for compliance with Islamic law. Their criteria largely reflect those adopted by the S&P, FTSE and the Dow Jones Islamic Indexes, although investment is also specifically prohibited in companies involved in meat production or sale where the animals are not slaughtered according to Islamic rites. As with the three international indexes, the Malaysian scholars focus on the core activities of the company and do not specify a percentage for excluding companies because of involvement in *haram* activities.

The SAC also adopts positive criteria for the *Shari'ah* screening of companies in Malaysia. The public perception or the image of the company must be good and its core activities should have importance to the Muslim *ummah* and the country. The company's guiding principles should conform to *maslahah*, the beliefs of Muslims. Companies that serve the non-Muslim community, usually the Chinese population in Malaysia, are regarded as legitimate recipients of investment, provided they do not conflict with that which is customarily accepted by Muslims.

Financial screening

The criteria for selection outlined above are essentially qualitative in the sense that they involve judgement rather than precise measurement. Quantitative criteria are, however, also used when screening equities to ensure that they are *Shari'ah* compliant. These involve calculation of ratios, such as the proportion of interest-bearing debt to assets or the ratio of total debt to the average market capitalisation of a company over a period of twelve months.

The issue of leverage is complicated. Ideally it would be desirable to avoid investing in companies which have any involvement with *riba*-based banks, but this would mean the exclusion of virtually all quoted companies, including those whose stocks are traded in the equity markets of Muslim countries. In practice, fund-management groups seeking to comply with *Shari'ah* adopt several criteria, and there is disagreement and debate about what approach is most appropriate. First, they examine the extent to which a company's income is derived from interest, any proportion in excess of 5 per cent being unacceptable. The second criterion is to consider the extent of debt-to-equity finance, a proportion in excess of one third being unacceptable. Rushdi Siddiqui, the founder of the Dow Jones Islamic Indices, advocated tighter criteria with a limit of 25 per cent for the debt-to-capitalisation ratio, but there was no consensus on this.

The FTSE index adopts only one financial screen, excluding companies whose interest-bearing debt divided by assets is equal or greater than one third or 33.33 per cent. The Dow Jones Islamic Indexes have three financial screens to exclude companies:

1. no Islamic investment if total debt divided by the trailing twelve-month average market capitalisation is greater than or equal to 33 per cent;
2. omit companies if the sum of cash and interest-bearing securities divided by the trailing twelve-month average market capitalisation is greater than or equal to 33 per cent of revenues;
3. exclude companies if the accounts receivable divided by total assets are greater than or equal to 45 per cent of revenues.

Problems and potential injustices with financial screening

Although those who advocate financial screening are well intentioned, it can have unfortunate consequences both for the companies included in an Islamic equity portfolio and the Muslim investors in the fund. In bear markets such as those experienced in most Western countries in 2001–2, and even more dramatically in 2007–8, market capitalisation can fall significantly while debt remains constant or rises. This results in many additional companies excluded under the first financial screen criteria, and in the case of the post-2001 slump, high technology companies that had been much favoured by the Islamic fund management industry were soon excluded. Having a trailing twelve-month average for market capitalisation delays exclusion, but when bear markets persist, the inevitable occurs. However, such was the depth and duration of the 2007–8 equity price falls, the leveraging criteria were relaxed, and this was approved by the *Shari'ah* boards of the index providers, as although there was a reluctance to take such action, it was viewed as a necessity dictated by the adverse market developments.

It is debatable if excluding companies because of cyclical developments affecting the entire market is justified, or indeed whether it is really legitimate to include debt-laden companies simply because there has been a bull market with a very positive impact on their market capitalisation. These matters deserve further consideration from *Shari'ah* scholars, as companies cannot be blamed or excused because of developments in the market in general, although admittedly it can be argued that prudent companies with low or moderate debt are less likely to be affected by market downturns than those with high debt. Nevertheless, Islamic disinvestments during a slump may make matters worse for a struggling company, and bring bankruptcy and redundancy for employees, including those who are Muslims. Investors in the Islamic equity fund may also suffer, as selling shares when prices are falling may not be the best exit strategy.

The FTSE Islamic Index does not screen out companies with more than one third of their revenues deriving from interest on cash and securities, but the Dow Jones Islamic Indexes, as already indicated, specifically exclude such companies, as does S&P. This exclusion of course applies to most conventional banks, but arguably there is no need to use a financial screen to exclude these institutions, as they are excluded in any case because of the sector screen.

Investment companies may be excluded if they have excessive cash holdings under this financial screen, as in practice their liquidity is likely to be invested in interest-earning bank accounts or conventional bonds. For specifically Islamic investment companies the answer to the liquidity dilemma will be ultimately to hold sovereign and corporate *sukuk* when they become more widely issued and traded. For conventional investment companies such securities are likely to remain marginal for their liquidity management.

For any prudently managed investment company it is sensible to hold more liquidity in volatile and uncertain market conditions, especially when equity prices are falling. Conversely when market prices are rising, it makes sense to use cash to purchase equities so that Muslim investors in the fund will benefit from the capital gains. In other words, holdings of cash and interest-bearing securities vary according to the business cycle, and imposing fixed ceilings on such holdings may not always be helpful to either Muslim investors or the managers of investment companies who are only trying to act responsibly. Again this criterion for exclusion may need further consideration by *Shariʻah* scholars.

The concern of the *Shariʻah* advisors to the Dow Jones Islamic Indexes over receivables arises because there is often interest charged on deferred payments and accounts overdue. The stipulation that companies should be excluded if the ratio of accounts receivable to total assets exceeds 45 per cent is designed to ensure that companies selected for Islamic portfolios are not dependent on interest income for most of their earnings. However, this is exactly what has happened to many multinational industrial companies that might otherwise be suitable for inclusion in Islamic fund portfolios. Due to the global competition in the vehicle industry for example, car manufacturers such as Ford and General Motors have become in effect banks, with most of their profits derived from financing vehicle sales through extended payments terms.[7] None of these manufacturers now qualify for inclusion in the Dow Jones Islamic Indexes, even though they are the world's largest car manufacturing companies.

Rather than specifying a fixed proportion for income

from cash and interest-bearing securities or a limit on receivables the FTSE Islamic Index suggests that Muslim investors can purify their income through dividend cleansing. This implies giving away any income derived from *haram* sources to charitable causes, and hence making the residual income *halal*. The so-called tainted dividend receipts relate to the portion, if any, of a dividend paid by a constituent company in an Islamic equity portfolio that is attributable to activities that are not in accordance with *Shari'ah* law. Once this is calculated, Muslim investors have the opportunity to legitimise their earnings, and deserving charities benefit.

Lessons from the ethical-investment industry

As already indicated, there are parallels between the concerns of investors involved with the ethical-investment industry in the West and those who entrust their money to Islamic equity funds. As with Islamic equity-fund management the ethical industry uses both positive and negative screens for stock selection. The major difference is that the screens are socially determined rather than through religious teaching. Often the ethical industry is described as socially responsible investing, the main concerns being matters of social conscience and environmental issues. Although the ethical-investment industry is primarily driven by secular concerns, and does not promote an overtly religious message, some of the leading participants such as Friends Provident and Clerical Medical in the United Kingdom have Christian origins, the former being associated with the Society of Friends, popularly known as the Quakers as being God fearing they quaked in His sight.

The Friends Provident Stewardship Fund is the leading United Kingdom ethical fund. It was established in 1984 and in November 2011 was valued at £213 million ($370 million) compared to $220 million under management in the AlAhli Global Trading Equity Fund, the largest Islamic fund. Friends Provident Stewardship Fund aims to avoid companies that cause environmental damage and pollution or are involved in the manufacture and sale of weapons, trade with or have operations in oppressive regimes, are involved in exploitation of developing countries, unnecessary exploitation of animals, nuclear power, tobacco or alcohol production, gambling, pornography or offensive or misleading advertising. As most Muslim economies are developing, and some have oppressive regimes, the negative list of the Friends Provident Stewardship Fund may be of particular interest to Islamic equity-fund managers and their *Shari'ah* advisors. It is noteworthy that the Friends Provident Stewardship Fund excludes investment companies involved in alcohol production and any investment in the gaming industry.[8]

Islamic Equity Funds should arguably stress more the positive criteria for selecting companies rather than simply listing prohibitions. The Friends Provident Stewardship Fund looks to support companies that supply the basic necessities of life and provide high-quality products and services that are of long-term benefit to the community. As Muslims share these objectives that are stressed in Islamic teaching, it may be appropriate for Islamic Equity Funds to include such positive statements in their prospectuses. Other positive attributes that the Friends Provident Stewardship Fund looks for in companies include a good record on the conservation of energy and natural resources, environmental improvements and pollution control, good relations with customers and suppliers, fair employment practices including a commitment to training and education, strong community involvement, an equal opportunities policy and openness about company activities. Again most investors seeking *Shari'ah* compliance support such objectives.

At present the Islamic equity funds industry is largely reactive, disinvesting when companies breach its financial screens or change the nature of their business, hence being excluded by the sector screens. The ethical investment industry is more proactive than reactive, seeking to engage with companies in order to change their policies, so that they can conform to their social and environmental agendas. In other words, they use their financial muscle to encourage positive change.

The Friends Provident Stewardship Fund has adopted a policy involving a 'Responsible Engagement Overlay' (*reo*®) that aims to encourage companies to be more responsive to society's expectations of them. In particular it has two approaches, the first being 'to encourage companies to adopt appropriate and credible corporate policies and practices relevant to their sector including the adoption of internationally recognised codes and standards'. The second approach is 'to promote the benefits of assessing the business risks relating to human rights as part of a company's overall risk management evaluation process'.

In practice, most of the engagement with companies by the Friends Provident Stewardship Fund has involved encouraging international pharmaceutical companies to supply patented medicines to the developing world at lower prices and improve working conditions and employment practices. There has also been an initiative to encourage companies involved in Southern Africa to address the issue of HIV/AIDS in the workplace.

The Friends Provident Stewardship Fund has identified four benefits for companies from adopting policies of social responsibility. First, it enhances company reputation and protects brands. Second, there is a reduced risk of legal action and consumer protest. Third, there is protection of employees, supply chains and market position. Finally, such policies should result in improved employee recruitment, retention and motivation.

Unlike many fund management groups, the Friends Provident Stewardship Fund is actively engaged in corporate governance by voting in around 1,500 companies each year. Where they vote against a company proposal, reasons are given in writing and the Fund attempts to start a discussion with the company over its concerns. The complete voting record is made available on the website and updated every month. Successful examples of engagement include that with GlaxoSmithKline over the health crisis in emerging markets; reorganisation of the management of Intercare, a medical product company, so that the posts of Chairman and CEO were separated; revised wood sourcing policies by Travis Perkins so that forestry sustainability was promoted; and new training policies by Citigroup so that employees were made aware of the potential implications of their financing decisions for the environment and social risk.

The ethical-investment industry encompasses stock broking and portfolio management as well as equity-fund management, Holden and Partners being the largest specialist firm in the sector in the United Kingdom.[9] Individuals with more than £100,000 ($178,000) to invest can have a personal ethical screening service, and Holden and Partners also offer ethical pensions and investment opportunities for venture capital. The standard of information disclosure to clients is extremely high, and in many ways could be regarded as a benchmark for the Islamic fund-management industry.

Holden and Partners offers their clients three different levels of ethical compliance, designated light green, medium weighting and dark green. Even for the light-green designation companies are excluded that are involved in tobacco production or distribution, the armaments trade, animal testing or environmental exploitation. However, much of the emphasis is on positive screening. Portfolios are designed to have market-sector weightings, so that performance can be compared with major indices, but companies for inclusion are selected according to a best-of-sector approach, this being defined in ethical rather than financial terms. Companies are selected that exemplify the best environmental and social policy in each sector.

For Holden and Partners the medium ethical category implies some exposure in oil, pharmaceuticals and banks, but below market weight for each of these sectors. Companies that are included in the dark-green portfolio are expected to contribute significantly to the ethical objectives adopted, with, for example, waste management companies making a major contribution to recycling.

Although many may view *Shari'ah* compliance in binary terms of *haram* and *halal*, there are often ethical trade-offs when adopting screening and choices are by no means clear cut. It is not simply a matter of sacrificing material gain in order to be certain that Islamic principles are being upheld, but of recognising that a step-by-step approach may be the best means of attaining religious objectives. Hence, those who are at the light-green stage may be regarded as being at the start of the journey, and those at the dark-green stage further down the road. There are philosophical as well as practical lessons for the Islamic screening process to be learnt from the ethical screening experience. Yusuf Talal DeLorenzo, a leading *Shari'ah* advisor to numerous equity-fund managers, has stressed the benefits of building bridges between the ethical and Islamic investment industries.[10]

Widening the remit for *Shariʿah* screening

Developing sound and acceptable screens is crucial for both Islamic and ethical finance. It reduces the workload of the *Shariʿah* board, as once the criteria are agreed, fund managers can simply apply the rules and exclude *haram* stock. Many institutions offer a wide range of Islamic equity funds as clients have different time horizons and risk preferences, and it would be impossible for *Shariʿah* board members to advise on every single stock purchase by fund managers. The availability of standardised screens can therefore facilitate the development of the industry. For example, the National Commercial Bank of Saudi Arabia introduced new products such as the Islamic Equity Builder Certificates without increasing the workload on their *Shariʿah* advisors, as fund managers simply apply the screening software supplied by the Dow Jones Islamic Indexes.[11]

Satisfying the *Shariʿah* advisors regarding screening is a necessary but not a sufficient condition for the success of Islamic equity funds. Having a *Shariʿah* committee composed of eminent and respected scholars is a source of comfort for most clients, and is a major factor in ensuring a sound reputation for the fund. However, knowledgeable clients in the future may want direct assurance of *Shariʿah* compliance rather than indirect assurance through the *Shariʿah* committee as intermediaries. As with ethical funds clients may wish to make their own judgements in the light of full information on the screens, and an explanation of why they are relevant to *Shariʿah* compliance. This will not necessarily reduce the role of the *Shariʿah* advisors, but rather they may become more communicators and educators as well-informed clients ask ever more questions about the rationale for investing according to conscience and not simply on the basis of financial returns.[12]

Legislation and the IFSB guidelines on Islamic collective investment schemes

There is no legislation specifically pertaining to Islamic funds but they are subject to laws on fund licensing and issuance. For example, in Malaysia the Capital Markets and Services Act of 2007 provides the legal framework for managed funds, the majority of which are *Shari'ah* compliant. In Malaysia it is the Securities Commission which has responsibility for managed funds and in Saudi Arabia their equivalent is the Capital Markets Authority. The latter has a mutual-funds department which licences funds in the Kingdom in accordance with Article 39 of the Capital Markets Law of 2004. Malaysia and Saudi Arabia are the two major jurisdictions for Islamic funds, with 167 funds offered in Saudi Arabia with assets under management worth $18 billion and 178 funds offered in Malaysia worth $9.5 billion. There are 746 Islamic funds worldwide worth $49 billion, with Saudi Arabia accounting for 37 per cent of the total.[13]

Although there have been few initiatives at national level of relevance to Islamic funds the work of the IFSB at the international level may prompt more interest as it identifies many of the issues and provides a benchmark for future action. The *IFSB Guiding Principles on Islamic Collective Investment Schemes* were issued in January 2009 in order to establish a framework for Islamic funds to be regulated and managed in accordance with *Shari'ah* rules.[14] The document draws on the International Organisation for Securities Commission Organisations (IOSCO) principles and seeks to apply these to Islamic funds.[15] The *IFSB Guiding Principles* provide for portfolio screening to ensure investment portfolios are *Shari'ah* compliant and the purification of tainted income, including interest, through its donation to charitable causes.[16] As with investment *mudaraba* accounts the IFSB suggests that Islamic funds can establish profit-equalisation reserves to smooth return to investors.[17]

Many investors in Islamic funds, in common with those investing in conventional mutual funds, witnessed the value of their assets decrease substantially as a result of the global financial crisis of 2008. The absence of exposure to conventional banks mitigated some of the losses of the Islamic funds, but they could not escape the effect of the recession on *Shari'ah*-compliant businesses. The Islamic mutual-fund sector is slowly reviving, and is better placed than previously given the attention that has been paid to regulatory issues. Although the IFSB guiding principles cannot revive Islamic collective-investment schemes, they should help to ensure that the quality of provision improves. This can undoubtedly contribute to the long-term development of the industry.

Notes

1. S. M. Hasanuzzaman, *Islam and Business Ethics* (London: Institute of Islamic Banking and Insurance, 2003), pp. 80–2.
2. Nublan Zaky Yusoff, *An Islamic Perspective of Stock Markets* (Kuala Lumpur: Dian Darulnaim Sdn. Bhd., 1992), pp. 137–45.
3. www.djindexes.com/jsp/islamicMarketOverView.jsp.
4. Muhammad Nejatullah Siddiqi, *Partnership and Profit-Sharing in Islamic Law* (Leicester: The Islamic Foundation, 1985), pp. 17–18.
5. The Jordan Islamic Bank pioneered specified investment accounts from the early 1980s.
6. www.islamic-finance.net/islamic-equity/tii.html.
7. Graeme Maxton, 'A rough road', in 'The World in 2004', *The Economist*, London, 2003, pp. 119–20.
8. Friends Provident, *Stewardship Criteria and Policies* (London: Friends Provident, 2011), pp. 9–11.

9. www.holden-meehan.co.uk.

10. Yusuf Talal DeLorenzo, *Shariah Supervision of Islamic Mutual Funds*, paper presented to the Fourth Harvard Islamic Finance Forum, October 2000, p. 6.

11. www.alahali.com/ib/investing/islamicfunds.

12. Rodney Wilson, 'Screening criteria for Islamic equity funds', in Sohail Jaffer (ed.), *Islamic Asset Management: Forming the Future for* Shari'ah *Compliant Investment Strategies* (London: Euromoney Books, 2004), pp. 35–45.

13. Data from Islamic Finance Information Service, London, 4 November 2011.

14. *IFSB Guiding Principles on Islamic Collective Investment Schemes* (Kuala Lumpur: IFSB, January 2009), 6.3, p. 2.

15. IOSCO, *Objectives and Principles of Securities Regulation* (Madrid: IOSCO, May 2003), Section 11, pp. 27–31.

16. *IFSB Guiding Principles on Islamic Collective Investment Schemes* (Kuala Lumpur: IFSB, January 2009), 41.2–3, p. 14.

17. Ibid. 59–61, p. 19.

CHAPTER 11
CORPORATE GOVERNANCE IN ISLAMIC FINANCIAL INSTITUTIONS

As stakeholder interests in Islamic financial institutions are distinctive from those of their conventional counterparts this has implications for corporate governance structures. The rights and obligations of the different stakeholder groups reflect two separate factors, first the participatory nature of Islamic finance, and secondly the need to have a body within the institution which can provide *Shari'ah* assurance. This applies not only in the case of Islamic banks, but also for *takaful* operators, fund managers and *Shari'ah*-compliant investment companies. The remit of this chapter extends to all of these categories of Islamic financial institution.

It is appropriate to address *Shari'ah* governance issues first as it is *Shari'ah* compliance that determines whether a financial institution can be categorised as Islamic. The issues include the responsibilities and duties of *Shari'ah* boards and their role in the governance structure, including consideration of the chain of accountability and how they report. In other words, the focus is on the procedures and methods for *Shari'ah* assurance.

The participatory nature of Islamic finance means that

governance is not solely about ensuring that shareholder interests are protected. Other stakeholder groups are also important including the investment *mudaraba* depositors in Islamic banks. The questions addressed here include the rights and responsibilities of investment *mudaraba* account holders with Islamic banks and how these relate to the interests of shareholders, given that there are potential conflicts between these different stakeholder groups. Whereas in Islamic banking conflicts of interest are managed through the governance structures, in *takaful* Islamic insurance, as indicated in Chapter 8, the aim is to provide financial segregation which prevents conflicts of interest arising in the first place. How this is achieved will also be examined here.

Principal and agent conflicts of interest in an Islamic context

The literature on corporate governance for Islamic financial institutions has only emerged recently and remains very limited, mostly in the form of reports from international organisations rather than independent academic studies. The pioneering work was by M. Umer Chapra and Habib Ahmed for the Islamic Research and Training Institute of the Islamic Development Bank in 2002.[1] Their paper explored how the principal agent problem applies to Islamic financial institutions, an issue which had already been discussed in relation to Islamic banking by John Presley and John Sessions in an article in the *Economic Journal* published in 1993.[2] Chapra and Ahmed identify the challenges facing Islamic banks as organisations that should adhere to high moral standards, stressing management responsibilities, especially for effective risk-control systems. *Shari'ah* governance systems are also considered and how this fits into the wider governance framework. Their study also included the first ever survey of corporate governance in Islamic financial institutions, which resulted in good practices being identified. This enabled the authors to devise a code of best practice which is appended to the study.

The first thoughtful academic contribution was by Mahmoud A. El Gamal, a Professor at Rice University in Houston, who advocated Islamic banks being organised as mutual societies rather than as listed companies with shareholders.[3] This would avoid the potential conflict of interest between shareholders and investment depositors. It would also be consistent with the vision for Islamic banking advocated by Islamic economists and the type of structures adopted in the early Islamic finance experiments in the 1960s in Egypt and Pakistan.

However, there has been a worldwide trend towards demutualisation in financial services, largely because of the constraints on mutual organisations raising capital for expansion. Essentially they have to turn to their members for capital contributions, whereas financial institutions which are listed on financial markets, including most major Islamic banks, can raise equity capital and call on their shareholders to subscribe to rights issues. Furthermore, because of listing requirements, the financial reporting by listed companies is usually more detailed and comprehensive than that for mutual societies. In practice mutual forms of organisation may be suitable for Islamic microfinance, but for Islamic commercial banking having a listing brings significant advantages.

Racha Ghayad has made a major contribution to the academic literature on corporate governance for Islamic banks by investigating its link to institutional performance.[4] Her doctoral thesis submitted to the University of Caen in France was on this topic, and a subsequent workshop presentation in Beirut based on her thesis was published in *Humanomics*, a journal which focuses on Islamic economics and finance. Ghayad believes that institutional performance for Islamic banks should not only be measured by financial indicators and ratios, but also by the quality of its *Shari'ah* governance system. In particular, investment *mudaraba* account holders not only value the returns they receive, but also derive satisfaction from their participation in Islamic banking activity and their identification with the institution. In principle, Racha Ghayad is correct in her analysis, which is based on survey interviews, but the problem is that qualitative variables cannot be measured, and the approach is inevitably impressionistic and value driven. This means that Islamic financial institutions cannot be meaningfully compared with each other or with their conventional counterparts. Financial ratios and other performance measures have their limitations, but they still provide objective yardsticks.

The other contributions to the corporate governance literature on Islamic finance have been in the form of brief articles or papers. Professor Bala Shanmugam and Vignesen Perumai of Monash University in Malaysia stressed how adherence to *Shari'ah* can address agency problems and then examined the models for *Shari'ah* governance in Malaysia, Bahrain, Saudi Arabia and Bangladesh.[5] Exactly how these models address agency problems is not explained, however, which limits the value of the article.

Nasser Suleiman, in his examination of corporate governance issues, focuses on the business culture within Islamic financial institutions and the responsibilities of employees to uphold Islamic values.[6] This will increase trust, and potentially reduce the operational risk resulting from employee malpractices or outright fraud. Furthermore, although Islamic banks have a duty to serve their clients, Suleiman believes that pious Muslims have a duty to use

Islamic financial institutions rather than *riba*-based banks if suitable services to cater for their financial requirements are being offered. In other words, the clients have stakeholder rights, but they, as well as potential clients, also have obligations to support the development of the Islamic finance industry.

Reports by international organisations on corporate governance in Islamic finance

The increasing research focus of international organisations on corporate governance issues relating to Islamic financial institutions has resulted in greater output in recent years than the academic contributions. Reports from the World Bank; the Organisation for Economic Cooperation and Development (OECD); Hawkamah, the Dubai-based corporate governance institute; and the Islamic Financial Services Board (IFSB) are reviewed in this section.

Wafiq Grais and Matteo Pellegrini, in an unusually controversial paper for the World Bank, explore some of the challenges in devising corporate governance systems for Islamic financial institutions.[7] They dispel the notion that just because these institutions are *Shari'ah* compliant their governance systems must be sound. They examine three cases of failure by Islamic financial institutions due to governance weaknesses, the first being BCCI which undertook to place funds obtained from Islamic banks into *Shari'ah*-compliant commodity trading, but in fact used the money for other purposes which were far from being Islamic. The second case was the collapse in 2001 of Ihlas Finance House, at that time Turkey's largest Islamic bank. Unknown to depositors most of their funds were misappropriated and lent to a small number of major shareholders. When the bank collapsed there were no assets remaining which could be used to reimburse the 200,000 depositors. The third failure was that of the Patni Cooperative Credit Society in India which took on excessive risks partly to compensate for the regulatory constraints under which it operated. It had to operate within the Cooperative Society Act which meant it could only operate within the state where it was licensed, yet at the same time it observed limitations on most of its business which resulted in it trying to spice up its portfolio at the margin to generate returns which were unsustainable.

Having reviewed corporate governance failures resulting in the collapse of Islamic financial institutions, Grais and Pellegrini suggest that because of their nature Islamic banks and *takaful* operators should be responsible to all their stakeholders and not simply their shareholders as with conventional banks. With conventional banks as with other listed companies, the main aim of management is to increase shareholder value. The interests of depositors and those being financed is primarily the responsibility of the regulatory authorities rather than the banks themselves, although of course the banks have to comply with regulatory demands in order to maintain their licences to operate. Assurance to customers regarding *Shari'ah* compliance is the responsibility of the Islamic financial institutions, as regulators may not be equipped to get directly involved in this. Grais and Pellegrini see *Shari'ah* compliance as essential for the ethical interests of all the stakeholders.

In addition, the special position of investment *mudaraba* depositors is stressed by Grais and Pellegrini. As the returns of these depositors are dependent on the performance of the Islamic financial institution they should have more stakeholder rights than conventional depositors, although not necessarily the equivalent to those of shareholders who are the owners. Grais and Pellegrini discuss this in terms of the stakeholders' financial interests. Clearly there has to be full transparency in the use of funds in the interests of all the stakeholders, and Grais and Pellegrini refer with approval to the Financial Accounting Standard 11 of the Accounting and Auditing Organisation for Islamic Financial Institutions (AAOIFI) in this respect.

Stijn Claessens of the World Bank, in a paper presented at a conference organised by the Islamic Financial Services Board in Kuala Lumpur in 2006, examines corporate governance issues in conventional banks and then contrasts the position of Islamic banks.[8] Like other commentators he focuses on the *Shari'ah* governance issue and the position of the *mudaraba* investment depositors, but he also examines the general institutional environment, which is often weaker in emerging Muslim economies. The World Bank has strongly emphasised the need for institutional capacity building in developing countries in recent years, an issue which also has implications for Islamic finance regulation and surveillance in poorer Muslim countries.

In the Middle East and North Africa region Hawkamah was established in 2005 to take the corporate governance agenda forward. Part of their work involved producing a policy brief on corporate governance for banks.[9] The section on *Shari'ah*-compliant banking covers not only the issues of *Shari'ah* governance and the rights of *mudaraba* investment depositors, but also raises the issue of clients being deceived if they deposit funds with an Islamic banking subsidiary of a conventional institution which then proceeds to use the funds for *riba*-based transactions. It is not suggested that this happens, but to avoid such an occurrence a firewall should be established between *Shari'ah*-compliant and conventional banking operations with no co-mingling of funds.

The IFSB has produced guiding principles on corporate governance for institutions offering Islamic financial services, primarily Islamic banks,[10] and separate guidelines for corporate governance for *takaful* operators and Islamic collective-investment schemes. The latter have already been considered in Chapters 8 and 10, respectively. Although the issues concerning corporate governance in relation to Islamic *mudaraba* account holders were first raised in AAOIFI deliberations in the 1990s, it was Simon Archer, a consultant to the IFSB, who drew attention to their position as stakeholders in relation to the shareholders.[11]

Shari'ah assurance mechanisms

Within Islamic financial institutions it has become good practice to establish a board that has the competency and resources to provide assurance that their operations are *Shari'ah* compliant. The first modern Islamic banks did not have formal *Shari'ah* assurance mechanisms, but since the late 1970s the appointment of an independent board of *Shari'ah* scholars has become the norm in jurisdictions where Islamic and conventional banks co-exist.

In jurisdictions where all banking must comply with *Shari'ah*, such as Iran, it is the national law which pro-vides the *Shari'ah* assurance, in Iran's case the 1983 Law on Usury-Free Banking. Hence, Bank Melli Iran does not have a *Shari'ah* board despite being the leading institution worldwide in terms of *Shari'ah*-compliant assets. Being state owned, the government is an important stakeholder, although its control is exercised through a High Council which determined policy priorities for all of Iran's nation-alised banks. Bank Melli's religious governance is evident from its code of ethics, which states under Section 1 that its employees, 'with absolute belief and confidence in the Almighty's Will, will strive to provide premium services, with customer satisfaction being the key priority'.[12] At the practical level, however, the financing products offered by

Bank Melli are similar to those offered by conventional banks, and although no designated interest is payable on domestic retail and business deposits or lending, the fee-and-reward structure is unremarkable. It seems that the governance structure ensures the 1983 law is implemented, but it does not provide a mechanism for ensuring that new financial products are *Shari'ah* compliant or encouraging the development of *Shari'ah*-based products.

Al Rajhi Bank, the leading Islamic bank in Saudi Arabia and the largest listed Islamic bank globally, has its own *Shari'ah* Board comprising six members. The founders of the bank mutually agreed in its memorandum of association in 1987 that all financial transactions should be subject to *Shari'ah*, and the remit of the Board is to ensure that this is the case. In particular, no financial product or service can be launched without the approval of the *Shari'ah* Board. The rules and procedures under which the *Shari'ah* Board operates were formalised in a charter in 1999 which was approved by the eleventh General Assembly of the Al Rajhi Bank. This stipulated that all decisions made by the *Shari'ah* Board would be binding on the institution and its employees. The *Shari'ah* Board has taken over 800 decisions since the bank's inception and these are recorded in the *Shari'ah* Monitoring Guide and *Shari'ah* Control Guidelines.[13] This provides the case law to which the *Shari'ah* Board can refer when making future decisions or when verifying the authenticity of existing contracts. The *Shari'ah* Board has appointed an executive committee which monitors the on-going operations of the bank. This consists of three members drawn from the *Shari'ah* Board, including the Secretary of the Board. It is the Executive Committee that updates the *Shari'ah* Monitoring Guide and *Shari'ah* Control Guidelines, and reports to the *Shari'ah* Board if there is any breach of its rulings.

Across the Gulf Co-operation Council (GCC) the remit and accountability of *Shari'ah* boards is similar to that of Al Rajhi Bank. Dubai Islamic Bank, the oldest Islamic bank in the world, dating from 1975, has a *Fatwa* and *Shari'ah* Supervisory Board comprising five members including the Chairman, Dr Hussein Hamid Hassan and the General Secretary, Dr Mohammed Abdul Hakim Zoeir, who is responsible for internal *Shari'ah* auditing. The duties of the Board are set out in Article 7 of the Bank's Memorandum and Articles of Association under clauses 74–84, with clause 78 specifying that the Board of Directors is obliged to obey the *fatwas*, irrespective of whether they result from a unanimous consensus of the *Shari'ah* Board members or a majority vote.[14] The *Shari'ah* Board issues a detailed report on its activities annually to the Board of Directors and provides a summary statement in the Bank's Annual Report certifying that its operations are *Shari'ah* compliant. Similar statements are issued by the *Shari'ah* board of Kuwait Finance House, the second-largest stock-market-listed Islamic bank, which has a *Shari'ah* Board of six members.[15]

The content of *Shari'ah* rulings is of course a separate matter to the governance structures, the central concern here. The lack of standardisation extends not only to *Shari'ah* rulings, but to the organisation of *Shari'ah* governance systems. As regulators have become involved in this, what have emerged are national systems, with significant variations between jurisdictions. The contrasts between Iran, which has a universal Islamic banking system, and the GCC countries, where conventional and Islamic financial institutions operate side by side, have already been noted. However, there are other variants, notably in Malaysia, where national *Shari'ah* boards have been established by both the Central Bank and the Securities Commission. Only these bodies have the authority to issue *fatwa*, with the remit of the *Shari'ah* boards of the individual banks confined to giving guidance on compliance with the national *fatwa*.

Governance to serve investment-account holders

The investment-account holders have a much greater stake in an Islamic bank than depositors with a conventional bank as they share in its profits rather than being paid interest. Profits depend on the Islamic bank's financial performance, whereas interest returns may depend on macroeconomic developments, including monetary policy considerations at central bank level. It is appropriate therefore that there should be more direct corporate responsibility to invest-ment-account holders in an Islamic bank which will be reflected in the corporate governance structure.

Furthermore, the legal contracts between the invest-ment-account holders are based on *mudaraba*, a principle under which the depositors have specific rights and duties. In particular, as financiers, *rabb al maal*, they have a right to a share of the profits of the Islamic bank, which the man-agement cannot override. Indeed their share of the profit is specified in the contract governing the *mudaraba* deposit, and cannot be changed once the contract is signed. Their claim on any profits generated depends on the size of their deposit and usually the period of withdrawal notice, with those whose deposit is subject to a longer period of notice earning more in recognition of their liquidity sacrifice.

In *mudaraba* contracts it is the *rabb al maal* as financier who is responsible for any losses and not the *mudarab*, the latter being the business manager or entrepreneur. When applied to Islamic bank *mudaraba* investment depositors the implication is that if their position is equated with the *rabb al maal*, they are liable for any losses, and not the bank management, who as the *mudarab*, risk losing their jobs in the event of the Islamic bank incurring losses. To have the management sharing losses would arguable be unjust, as they already have redundancy risk, and to penalise them further when they are losing their jobs would be exploitative.

Although the inherent justice to the parties in *mudaraba* contracts is evident, there are a number of considerations when applying these contracts to an Islamic banks' investment *mudaraba* deposits. First, there is the issue of bank management remuneration which is usually in the form of monthly salaries. These are determined by the board of directors without consultation with the investment *mudaraba* depositors, but raising salaries could raise bank operating costs and adversely affect the profit in which the *mudaraba* investment-account holders are sharing. Such conflicts of interest can be alleviated by paying the management a profit share in the form of bonuses. As *mudaraba* is a profit-sharing contract between the *rabb al maal* and the *mudarib*, insofar as the management plays the role of the latter, there is indeed a case for such sharing. In modern banking contracts, however, bonuses are often linked to individual rather than institutional performance, which can result in a favourable incentive structure, but can also result in abuse if doubtful performance criteria are introduced. This was all too evident in investment banking prior to the global financial crisis, although appears not to have been an issue in Islamic banking.

A second factor potentially compromising the integrity of investment *mudaraba* contracts for Islamic bank deposits is the organisation of Islamic banks as state-owned, public or private companies with shareholders. Under modern corporate governance arrangements it is the shareholders that are the owners, with all the rights and responsibilities that implies, and not the investment *mudaraba* depositors. The issue immediately arises of potential conflicts of interest between investment depositors and shareholders and how these might be resolved. If higher profits are paid to the investment *mudaraba* account holders this could be at the expense of the dividends paid to shareholders, for example, and conversely higher dividend payments could result in less profit being paid to investment *mudaraba* depositors.

There could also be potential injustices involving the investment *mudaraba* depositors' loss liability, as if they absorb losses by having the value of their deposits written down, this may protect the shareholders if there are lower reported losses, or even no losses. The price of shares are less likely to fall in these circumstances, resulting in shareholders enjoying potential upside capital gains, but having less risk of downside capital losses. In contrast, the investment *mudaraba* account holders cannot be given guarantees on their deposits under *Shari'ah* because of the profit- and loss-sharing obligations of those acting as *rabb al maal*, and hence there can be no element of investment protection.

Furthermore, the financial position of the investment *mudaraba* depositors is worse than that of the shareholders with respect to capital gains. As bank-account holders they cannot expect to have more than the nominal value of their deposits returned, which in inflationary conditions means a loss over time in the real value of their investments. In contrast, shareholders are more likely to see the real value of their investments maintained or even increased, and may view their shareholdings as a hedge against inflation. Their holding in the bank represents a share in a real asset, whereas investment *mudaraba* account holders are merely holding monetary assets.

In conventional corporate governance structures the concern is with conflicts of interest between managers and shareholders which can result in moral hazard and asymmetric information problems to the detriment of the latter.

Hence, there is a need for an independent chairman of the board of directors to represent shareholder interests and non-executive directors who are not involved in the management of the company. These corporate governance considerations also apply in the case of Islamic banks, but there is in addition the issue of who represents the interests of the investment *mudaraba* account holders. Should it be the board of directors, and if not, who else?

Establishing a separate body to represent the *mudaraba* account holders would compromise the authority of the board of directors and result in confusion over corporate governance responsibilities. The *mudaraba* account holders are not the owners of the Islamic bank and therefore cannot benefit from ownership rights. Only the shareholders have the right to vote on changes to the articles of association of an Islamic bank, or on the appointment or re-appointment of members of the board of directors and the company auditors. It is normally the board of directors which nominates the members of the *Shari'ah* board, and these appointments are usually approved at the annual general meetings which are attended by the shareholders. The investment-account holders are not allowed to attend the annual general meeting or any extraordinary meeting called by whatever proportion of shareholders is stipulated in the company's articles of association. Whether they should be given observer status is a debatable point. At least this would allow them to attend annual and extraordinary general meetings, but with no voting rights and perhaps no right to ask questions of the board.

Although there have not been any specific proposals for corporate governance changes to take account of the interests of *mudaraba* investment-account holders, the IFSB in their *Guiding Principles on Corporate Governance for Institutions Offering Only Islamic Financial Services,* have identified two issues that Islamic financial institutions should address. The first relates to the appetite for risk of *mudaraba* investment-account holders, which is similar to that of conventional savings depositors rather than equity investors.[16] The latter are prepared to risk their capital to obtain a higher return, through both dividends and capital gains. Although in the long term dividends matter, in the short run equity investors may be prepared to sacrifice dividends if there are the prospects of enhanced capital gains. In contrast, *mudaraba* investment-account holders expect to have their deposits returned in full, even though the principle cannot be guaranteed under *Shari'ah*, and in addition, they also expect a regular return on their investment rather like that accruing to conventional savings depositors. Hence, many Islamic banks have introduced the concept of profit smoothing, whereby not all of the profits are distributed to investment-account holders in years when returns are buoyant, but rather a proportion is paid into a reserve fund which can be used to make payouts to depositors in years when profits are low or losses are incurred. The decision on how much to pay out and the amount to add to reserves will have to be taken by the board of directors and reported to the shareholders, but there will not be a direct input from the investment-account holders themselves. There could potentially be a broader consultation, but depositors will not have an overview of the Islamic bank operations and will usually be less financially sophisticated than the shareholders. Therefore, reducing the rights of the shareholders by introducing such a consultation may not actually further the interests of the investment depositors in any case.

The second broader issue raised by the IFSB is the need for an Islamic financial institution to align its business strategy with the risk-and-reward stance of its clients, notably the investment-account holders.[17] There is the assumption that shareholders can take care of themselves, and can choose the risks they take, and sell their shares if necessary. While not wanting to undermine the loyalty of Islamic bank shareholders the IFSB stresses the special responsibility of Islamic bank managers and boards of directors towards their clients, including the investment-account holders. It even urges a 'know your client' policy to ascertain the risk-and-return expectations of Islamic investment-account holders.

The responsibility of Islamic banks to unrestricted Islamic investment-account holders is arguably greater than that to restricted account holders, with most of the discussion so far relating to the former. Whereas unrestricted Islamic account holders share in the bank's profits and have a legitimate interest in its performance, the bank merely acts as an agent for the restricted-account holders. The latter share in the profits of the project to which their funds are restricted, and therefore their main interest and involvement is with the project and not the bank. They merely pay the bank an arrangement fee for identifying the investment opportunity and an annual management charge for administering the profit-share payments and any additional capital subscriptions. Hence, the restricted-investment depositors cannot be regarded as stakeholders in the Islamic bank comparable to the unrestricted-account holders.

Corporate governance in *takaful*

Islamic insurance is based on the principle of risk sharing rather than risk transfers as is the case with conventional insurance. Two structures are widely employed as explained in Chapter 8, the first being the *wakala* model whereby the *takaful* operator receives a fee for managing the fund as agent or *wakeel*, but the policyholders themselves are the principals who control the fund. The alternative structure is a *mudaraba* arrangement which involves profit sharing between the operator as *mudarib* and the policyholders as *rabb al maal* or financiers, but with the policyholders responsible for any losses. In practice, potential losses are limited by the underwriting of the risk, with the re-*takaful* contracts based on the *wakala* principle where the underwriter is paid a fee.

The key corporate governance issue is defining the relationship between the insured and the *takaful* operators, who constitute the key stakeholders. The relationship will of course be different depending on whether the *wakala* or *mudaraba* model is used, as the responsibilities of an agent or *wakil* are different to those of the *mudarib*. Essentially, the latter, although they have to respect their contractual relations with the policyholders as financiers, have much more discretion in how they manage the *takaful* fund. They have a profit-sharing incentive to generate a surplus, which implies taking some investment risk with the funds they manage, subject to the fund being sufficiently solvent to meet ongoing claims. In contrast, the *wakil* will simply earn a fee, and even if there is a performance bonus, their priority is to safeguard the funds of the *takaful* contributors rather than acting in an entrepreneurial manner. The participants will have been motivated to have made their *tabarru* or donation to the fund because of social solidarity and the principle of mutual help. If the *wakil* mismanages the *takaful* funds, or loses the capital through taking excessive risks, then claims will not be covered and the social solidarity will have been undermined, perhaps even betrayed.

The implication of this is that under the *wakala* model, the *wakil* is more likely to prefer to invest in *sukuk*, *Shariʿah*-compliant equivalents to fixed-income investments, rather than equities which are subject to market risk. With *sukuk* the major risk is of default, but in the case of sovereign *sukuk* or issuances by highly rated business corporations the risk is minimal. As *sukuk* usually mature after less than five years and investors get the nominal value of their capital returned, such *sukuk* are appropriate assets for *takaful* operators providing vehicle or health cover. Those offering family *takaful*, which provides policies with a maturity length of twenty years or more, can take a long-term view of equity price movements and ride out the inevitable cycles in equity markets. Arguably it might be more appropriate to use a *mudaraba* structure for such *takaful* operations, in order to provide a long-term profit incentive for the managers. In terms of objectives family *takaful* resembles life insurance, with the policyholder's dependents receiving financial assistance in the event of premature death or major illness resulting in them no longer being able to work. If the policyholder survives until the *takaful* fund matures, they will then benefit from either a lump sum or a regular income as with a conventional endowment policy.

The *IFSB Guiding Principles on Governance for Islamic Insurance* was referred to in Chapter 8. They stress the importance of *takaful* operators having an appropriate code of ethics which covers issues such as providing clear advice to clients on the most suitable cover given their needs. They are also concerned with avoiding misleading marketing and selling or the duplicitous practices sometimes evident in conventional insurance. The IFSB recommend the establishment of a governance committee to oversee the workings of the *takaful* operator and its relationship with other stakeholders to ensure justice prevails. The committee could be comprised of a non-executive director, an actuary to provide technical guidance on contributions and claims, and a representative of the *Shari'ah* board to ensure morality prevails in all dealings while maintaining an appropriate balance between stakeholder interests.

The IFSB also recommends the implementation of appropriate policies for financial disclosures and ensuring that stakeholders have fair access to material and relevant information. Benefits should be clearly illustrated to clients drawing on realistic projection of likely future income in the case of long-term family *takaful*. *Takaful* operators should ensure that they have appropriate mechanisms in place to safeguard the solvency of the funds under their management. The operators should also have devised a sound investment strategy and prudently manage the assets and liabilities of the *takaful* fund to ensure future obligations can be met.

Fortunately there are an increasing number of examples of good governance practice in the *takaful* industry which should assure stakeholders. In Saudi Arabia, both banks and insurance operators compete for *takaful* business by stressing their sound governance principles. Bank AlJazira, a leading *takaful* provider in Saudi Arabia, uses a *wakala* model and stresses its principles of mutual responsibility, mutual co-operation and mutual protection.[18] SABB Takaful, an affiliate of Saudi Arabia British Bank which is part owned by HSBC, stresses the credibility of its *Shari'ah* committee and their role in reviewing and approving all products before they are made available to customers.[19] A detailed code of corporate governance has been introduced by Tawuniya, the leading insurance company in Saudi Arabia, originally established in 1985 as the National Company for Co-operative Insurance (NCCI).[20] Its corporate governance code covers the appointment and remit of the Board of Directors and the audit, executive, investment and business management committees. In Malaysia, the corporate governance report by Takaful Ikhlas includes information on the attendance of directors at board meetings, as well as the attendance record of members of the audit, nomination, remuneration and investment committees.[21]

Corporate governance for Islamic funds

Islamic funds with holdings screened for *Shari'ah* compliance have proved popular investment vehicles with many offered by banks, both conventional and Islamic, but an increasing number also provided by specialist investment companies. The funds can invest in listed or private equity, *sukuk* securities, real estate, commodities and even alternative investments including structured products, but only in one case a hedge fund, due to *Shari'ah* concerns about the legitimacy of short selling and the speculative nature of the latter. Some of the funds are open ended, with investors able to buy or sell units at any time. Others are close ended, usually with lock-in periods before capital can be redeemed.

Corporate governance concerns include the assurance to investors that the fund managers are acting in their best interests, procedures for *Shari'ah* compliance, disclosure of information on investment portfolios and the provision of regular and up-to-date information on fund performance. A bank offering Islamic funds may have the investments approved by its own *Shari'ah* board, or alternatively outsource compliance to a specialist company such as the Dow Jones Islamic Index. An investment company or dedicated fund provider may have its own *Shari'ah* board, as for example is the case with Jadwa, the leading wealth management group in Saudi Arabia. In its case the corporate secretary is responsible for corporate governance standards.[22]

The *IFSB Guiding Principles on Governance for Islamic Collective Investment Schemes* were briefly discussed in Chapter 10. They stress the importance of the disclosure of material information in an accurate and timely manner. The information should be presented in a way which is comprehensible for investors, or in other words in a format which is investor friendly. The governing body of the collective investment scheme has a duty to ensure that appropriate *Shari'ah* compliance mechanisms are in place, and much of the IFSB guidance focuses on this. There is also concern that movement of funds or assets into the collective investment scheme should be undertaken in a manner consistent with the best interests of the investors. Excessive buying or selling activity, referred to as churning, to increase brokerage fees would represent a malpractice, and would certainly be unethical and immoral. The IFSB stresses the need for transparency over management and other fees, and the provision of information on the smoothing of any dividend payments if this is fund policy. Unfortunately, during the global financial crisis of 2008 it became evident that many Islamic investment funds have been slow to release financial statements. Many investors in *Shari'ah*-compliant equity funds lost significant amounts, with the value of their investments declining by one third or more. In these circumstances the need for transparency is even more apparent.

Conclusions

It is encouraging that a framework is now in place for the corporate governance of Islamic financial institutions, and the IFSB in particular deserves to be commended for its efforts in this respect. Yet disclosure practice all too often remains inadequate, whether it is providing information to investment *mudaraba* depositors on how their profit shares are calculated, or reporting to investors in *Shari'ah*-compliant collective investment schemes in a timely manner. The exact role and workings of *Shari'ah* boards could also be

better explained, and it would be helpful if Islamic financial institutions had clear organisational charts, showing
the remit and accountability of their different stakeholder
groups. Despite the advances made, corporate governance
for Islamic financial institutions remains a work in progress.

Notes

1. M. Umer Chapra and Habib Ahmed, *Corporate Governance
   in Islamic Financial Institutions*, Islamic Research and
   Training Institute Occasional Paper No. 6 (Jeddah: Islamic
   Development Bank, 2002).

2. John R. Presley and John G. Sessions, 'Islamic economics: the
   emergence of a new paradigm', *Economic Journal*, 104, 1994,
   pp. 584–96.

3. Mahmoud A. El Gamal, *Islamic Finance: Law, Economics and
   Practice* (Cambridge: Cambridge University Press, 2006).

4. Racha Ghayad, 'Corporate governance and the global performance of Islamic banks', *Humanomics*, 24: 3, 2008,
   pp. 207–16.

5. Bala Shanmugam and Vignesen Perumai, 'Governance issues
   and Islamic banking', *Hedge Fund Monthly*, Singapore,
   December 2006, pp. 1–4.

6. Nasser M. Suleiman, 'Corporate government in Islamic
   Banks', see http://www.al-bab.com/arab/econ/nsbanks.htm.

7. Wafik Grais and Matteo Pellegrini, *Corporate Governance in
   Institutions Offering Islamic Financial Services*, World Bank
   Policy Research Working Paper 4052, Washington, November
   2006.

8. Stijn Claessens, 'Corporate governance of Islamic banks:
   why it is important, how it is special and what does that
   imply', paper presented to a Conference on Islamic Finance:
   Challenges and Opportunities (The World Bank Financial
   Sector Network and the Islamic Financial Services Board),
   Kuala Lumpur, 24 April 2006.

9. Elena Miteva and Nick Nadal, *Policy Brief by the Middle East and North Africa Taskforce on the Corporate Governance of Banks* (Paris: OECD/Dubai: Hawkamah, December 2007), p. 28 covers *Shari'ah*-compliant banking.

10. Islamic Financial Services Board, *Guiding Principles on Corporate Governance for Institutions Offering Only Islamic Financial Services (Excluding Islamic Insurance Takaful Institutions and Islamic Mutual Funds)*, Kuala Lumpur, December 2006.

11. Simon Archer, 'Islamic finance: opportunities, challenges and corporate governance issues', *World Bank Seminar*, Washington, 24 April 2006.

12. http://www.bmi.ir/En/BMICultural.aspx?smnuid=10015.

13. http://www.alrajhibank.com.sa/AboutUs/Pages/Shariaa Group.aspx.

14. http://www.alisalmi.ae/en/shariahboard_boardrules.htm.

15. Kuwait Finance House, *30th Annual Report*, 2008, p. 13.

16. Islamic Financial Services Board, *Guiding Principles*, p. 7.

17. Ibid. p. 8.

18. Bank AlJazira, *Takaful Taawuni*, see http://www.takaful.com.sa/home.asp.

19. SABB Takaful, see http://www.sabbtakaful.com.

20. Tawuniya, *Corporate Governance*, Riyadh, 2007. See http://www.tawuniya.com.sa/AboutUs/OurCompany.aspx.

21. Takaful Ikhlas Sdn. Bhd., *Directors Report and Audited Financial Statements*, Kuala Lumpur, 31 March 2008, pp. 3–7.

22. http://www.jadwa.com/about/pages/shariah-committee.aspx.

CHAPTER 12

PLURALITY, DIVERSITY AND POST-ARAB SPRING ISLAMIC FINANCE POSSIBILITIES

From this work it is evident that there is much plurality and diversity in Islamic finance. Law making is about establishing rules and sound regulation involves consistency in the treatment of the institutions being regulated. In other words, laws and regulation are concerned with establishing and maintaining standards. In any new industry there is considerable diversity, however, and Islamic finance is no exception. Although the term 'Islamic financial system' is often used, in reality there are many systems with much variation both between and indeed within jurisdictions.

There are inevitably calls for standardisation, as endless variety of practice can cause confusion and possibly even bring financial anarchy. On the other hand, variety brings choice and encourages innovation, both in the financial products offered and in how they are delivered. Islamic law is, quite rightly, morally prescriptive, but it can be flexible, and there are different paths to attaining *maqasid al shariah*, the objectives of Islamic law. It should be noted that the stress is on objectives, and not objective in the singular. Different scholars may stress different objectives, and in the early years of Islam different schools of *fiqh* emerged, with the Hanafi, Shafi'i, Malaki and Hanbali schools within the Sunni tradition and the Jafari school within the Shia tradition. The scholars serving on the *Shari'ah* boards of Islamic financial institutions come from all these traditions and schools, and although there are doctrinal differences between and within boards, this has not impeded progress or the issuance of *fatwa* on financial conduct.

Islam is not a centralised religion, and in the field of Islamic finance there are two international bodies, the International Islamic *Fiqh* Academy, associated with the Organisation of Islamic Cooperation, and the AAOIFI *Shari'ah* board which issues standards that are widely recognised. There has been no attempt to merge the two bodies, and even though there are different and sometimes conflicting *fatwa*, this does not appear to be adversely affecting the Islamic finance industry.

Restoring the influence of Al Azhar

Al Azhar University in Cairo, the oldest centre of Islamic scholarship, was marginalised from developments in Islamic finance during the Sadat and Mubarak eras, and its rector, Sheikh Mohammed Tantawi, declared that interest did not constitute *riba*, and that the interest charged and paid by banks in Egypt was legitimate, a position rejected by all the scholars serving on the *Shari'ah* boards of Islamic financial institutions. Tantawi died in 2010, less than one year before the Arab Spring, and Mubarak appointed his successor, Sheikh Ahmed Mohamed el-Tayeb. Since the Arab Spring, however, despite the earlier pronouncement by Tantawi, the *Shari'ah* scholars involved in Islamic finance have been made more welcome by the *ulama* at Al Azhar.

The Freedom and Justice Party, the moderate Islamist party that is expected to play a leading role in the new democratically elected government of Egypt, wants to restore Egypt's influence in the Arab and wider Muslim world. In the financial sphere, although Egypt lacks money, the *ulama* at Al Azhar can restore their influence by facilitating and encouraging the spread of Islamic finance, a relatively costless exercise. The rise of Cairo as a new hub for research and scholarship in Islamic finance will increase diversity and debate, especially on issues of how Islamic banks can reduce financial exclusion, a topic that received little attention from those involved in the industry in the oil-rich Gulf.

Legislation, regulation and political interference with Islamic finance in Egypt

Egypt was the location of the first modern Islamic financing experiment in 1963 when the Mit Ghamr Savings Bank was started, a *Shariʿah*-compliant credit union in which members would place *qard hasan* deposits in exchange for the right to interest-free loans. Over 358,000 accounts were opened in Mit Ghamr by 1970, clearly indicating its outstanding success in appealing to the Egyptian rural masses.[1] This early experiment was closed down by the authorities who preferred to see a state-controlled banking system with finance allocated in a manner consistent with government development priorities rather than through uncontrolled local initiatives, which had the potential to emerge as alternative centres of economic power, especially if the process of capital accumulation was influenced by Islamist ideals.[2]

Sadat, like his predecessor Nasser, knew little about Islamic finance but was mistrustful of Islamists. Nevertheless, following the passing of the Open Door Legislation to encourage foreign investment, the Gulf was seen as a potential source of capital. *Shariʿah*-compliant investment was viewed as a potentially significant component of that capital. Hence, in response to lobbying by advocates of Islamic finance, law number 48 of 1977 was passed permitting the establishment of Islamic banks and their regulation by the Central Bank of Egypt.[3] Both Prince Mohammed bin Faisal and Sheikh Saleh Abdullah Kamel, a wealthy Saudi business man and chairman of the Dallah al Baraka Group, proceeded to line up associates in Egypt to establish Islamic banks.

The Faisal Islamic Bank of Egypt obtained a licence from the Central Bank of Egypt on 14 June 1979, shortly followed by Al Baraka Bank of Egypt which was awarded its licence on 8 May 1980. A significant amount of capital was raised in the Gulf for these banking ventures, with Prince Mohammed bin Faisal taking a 20.25 per cent stake himself in the Faisal Bank, a financial inflow that seemed unaffected by the Arab financial boycott of Egypt following its peace treaty with Israel.[4] Just a few weeks later, a wholly locally owned competitor was established, Al Watany Bank of Egypt, that received a licence on 26 May 1980. Although Al Watany was established as a conventional bank, it offers Islamic retail-financing products.

Despite law number 48 being silent on specific Islamic issues, it provided autonomy from interference from government bodies apart from the Central Bank. Islamic banks, like their conventional counterparts, were required to maintain adequate cash-to-deposit ratios to cover likely liquidity requirements. However, the Central Bank of Egypt did not get involved in *Shari'ah* compliance issues. Islamic banks were free to include provisions for *Shari'ah* compliance in their own articles of association, with for example, Article 3 of the Faisal Islamic Bank's statutes referring to the prohibition of *riba* and the obligation to pay *zakat*.[5]

The absence of adequate legal and regulatory provision for Islamic finance created significant problems as voids soon get exploited. In addition to licensed banks, a number of Islamic investment companies were established in the 1980s, the largest of which was the Al-Rayyan Company. These were unregulated and functioned informally, but as they offered investors very high returns, they attracted large amounts of funds. Unfortunately their founders and managers were unable to identify high-yielding investments, and they were soon tempted into using new funds deposited to enhance the payout to existing investors, a practice that was unsustainable, indeed morally dubious and not the type of behaviour which might be expected from institutions marketing themselves as Islamic.[6] Inevitably these companies collapsed, and as they were unregulated, the investors lost most of their funds, and there was no question of the Central Bank of Egypt becoming involved in any compensation arrangements. There is little doubt that this experience resulted in lasting damage to the reputation of Islamic finance in Egypt, and was unhelpful for the expansion of the licensed Islamic banks.[7]

Although there has been over three decades of Islamic banking experience in Egypt, the laws governing Islamic banking remain unsatisfactory. In particular, law number 88 of 2003, the most recent version of the Banking Law, contains no provision for Islamic finance. Some of the articles are unhelpful, including Article 40 governing interest rates, Article 56(e) on reserves that has no reference to *Shari'ah* compliance, Article 59 which provides for interest penalties if banks fail to meet liquidity requirements and Article 87 providing for deposit protection. Investment *mudaraba* accounts cannot of course be guaranteed, as already indicated in Chapter 3, as otherwise the profit returns for risk sharing would be undermined.

In practice, the Central Bank of Egypt has adopted a flexible approach to the regulation of Islamic banking, although it has not been as closely involved in international regulatory debates in such an intense manner as the Central Bank of Bahrain or Bank Negara Malaysia, institutions that have done much to promote their own countries as international centres for Islamic finance. Egypt had no such ambitions, but the Central Bank is a full member of the Islamic Financial Services Board (IFSB), the Kuala Lumpur-based organisation that advises on the regulation of Islamic finance and produces prudential standards. Furthermore, on 18 and 19 January 2011, just before the popular uprising, the Central Bank of Egypt hosted an IFSB Workshop at the Egyptian Banking Institute. Plans for a *sukuk* issuance were announced in September 2011 as the caretaker government did not want to raise finance from the International Monetary Fund, but rather attract capital from regional sources.

Post-Arab Spring possibilities

It will be many years before the political and economic consequences of the Arab Spring will be fully apparent, however, the developments are viewed as encouraging for many proponents of Islamic finance. As Islamic banking has grown as a result of popular support, revolutions that have empowered the masses are seen as helpful for the industry. Democracies respond to popular movements, and it is evident that there are potential votes for any political party that includes in its agenda legal and regulatory changes to facilitate Islamic finance.

The former autocratic rulers justified their repressive methods by referring to the threat from so-called Islamic extremists. Islamic finance represents a very different face of religion, however, and far from being negative, its advocates engage peaceably in debates about how morality is needed in financial systems. Crony capitalism and the corruption and inequalities that inevitably arise in such a system are no longer acceptable by the masses in the Arab world. Evidence from Tunisia, Egypt and Libya suggests that Islamist political parties are popular because they stress honesty and condemn corrupt practices. They advocate respect for *Shari'ah* law rather than its imposition on everyone, which can prove divisive. In other words, in the banking field Islamist parties in the Arab world want to see legislation and regulation that facilitates Islamic finance, but not the forced conversion of the entire financial system as in Iran. The stress is on financial evolution, not revolution.

International challenges

At the international level there is also much criticism of the immorality of banking practice, the remuneration of bank chief executives and the asymmetric treatment of risk, with executives highly paid even when banks are failing and require taxpayer funds to remain solvent. As a fundamental Islamic financial principle is loss as well as profit sharing supporters of such a system can contribute to the global debate on banking reform.

Three predominately Muslim countries, Saudi Arabia, Turkey and Indonesia, are members of the G20 forum comprising the world's leading economies. It is the G20 which oversees the work of the International Monetary Fund and banking regulation through the Bank for International Settlement, including the endorsement of the Basel III standards. Although the G20 Muslim-majority countries have not been directly affected by the Arab Spring, they are well placed to voice the aspirations of young Muslims, including those who participated in the Arab uprisings, to the wider international community. In Islamic finance advocacy of an international level playing field for Islamic banks, *takaful* and Islamic capital market products could be very helpful. There will be an excellent opportunity to raise concerns about the equitable legal and regulatory treatment of Islamic finance internationally when the turn comes for each of these Muslim-majority countries to act as hosts for the G20 meetings, starting with Turkey's presidency in 2015.

Notes

1. Elias Kazarian, *Finance and Economic Development: Islamic Banking in Egypt*, Lund Economic Studies 45 (Lund: Lund University, 1991), p. 146.

2. Monzer Kahf, 'Islamic banks: the rise of a new power alliance of wealth and *shari'ah* scholarship', in Clement Henry and Rodney Wilson (eds), *The Politics of Islamic Finance* (Edinburgh: Edinburgh University Press, 2004), p. 19.

3. Rodney Wilson, *Islamic Banking and Finance in North Africa: Past Development and Future Potential* (Tunis: African Development Bank, 2011), pp. 23–4.

4. Gil Feiler, *Economic Relations Between Egypt and the Gulf Oil States, 1967–2000: Petro Wealth and Patterns of Influence* (Brighton: Sussex Academic Press, 2003), pp. 218–19.

5. Ahmed Abdel Fattah El Ashker, *The Islamic Business Enterprise* (London: Croom Helm Books, 1987), pp. 115–16.

6. Sami Zubaida, 'The politics of the Islamic investment companies in Egypt', *British Society for Middle Eastern Studies Bulletin*, 17: 2, 1990, pp. 152–61.

7. Charles Tripp, *Islam and the Moral Economy: the Challenge of Capitalism* (Cambridge: Cambridge University Press, 2006), p. 144.

amanah   a contract under which an object or a bank deposit is held on trust

arboun   a forward purchase by paying a deposit for a commodity to be delivered at a future date with the balance paid on delivery

daman   a contract providing a guarantee

fatwa   ruling by a scholar of Islamic jurisprudence such as those serving on the *Shari'ah* boards of Islamic financial institutions

fiqh   Islamic jurisprudence

gharar   legal uncertainty such as contractual ambiguity which could result in one of the parties to a contract exploiting the other

Hadith   sayings and deeds of the Prophet including when he was asked to provide a ruling on disputes

halal   permissible under Islamic law by being *Shari'ah* compliant

ijara   an operational leasing contract where the owner responsibilities justifies the payment of rent

ijtihad   the interpretation by a trained scholar, such as those serving on the *Shari'ah* boards of Islamic financial institutions, of how *Shari'ah* should be applied in new circumstances. This would apply, for example, to the consideration of what forms of activity are not permissible in complex modern financial markets. The interpretation involves examining the teaching of the Quran and the Hadith, as well as the study of *fiqh*, but previous *fatwa* are not necessarily relevant to changed conditions

istisna'a a sale contract that requires the manufacture of a good or the construction of a facility to exact specifications that are stipulated before the work commences. The financier, usually an investment bank, pays the raw material and wage costs of the supplier or contractor. On completion, after the contractor is paid the bank is reimbursed, the amount including an agreed predetermined profit margin. This type of contract is often used for project finance

maisir a game of chance involving gambling. Activities such as spread betting in financial markets are prohibited under *Shari'ah* as they are regarded as addictive and contribute nothing to society or an economy

mudaraba a partnership contract between an investor, the *rabb al maal*, and a business manager, the *mudarib*, which provides for profit sharing, with the *rabb al maal* receiving a return on their financial investment while the *mudarib* receives a share of the profit assessed on the basis of the value of their effort. The *rabb al maal* is sometimes regarded as a 'sleeping' partner as they do not get directly involved in business decisions after the initial contract is signed. Only the *rabb al maal* has a liability for any losses, as they are the sole provider of the capital. If there is no profit or a loss the *mudarib* will not receive any remuneration, but they have no further liability provided they are not negligent in their duties as defined in the original contract

murabaha   a sale contract whereby an Islamic financial institution sells a good to a client who makes deferred payments including a profit markup. The Islamic financial institution may have already acquired the good, or may acquire the good from the supplier on behalf of the client once the contract is signed

musharaka   a partnership contract between investors whereby they obtain predetermined shares in any profits generated. The partners take an active role in management, the extent of that activity being defined in the contract. If some partners agree to play a more active role than others, they may receive an enhanced profit share. Any losses are apportioned according to the capital contributions, as these indicate the capacity to take a hit

qard hasan   an interest-free loan, the only type of loan agreement permissible under *Shari'ah*. Although Islamic financial institutions cannot profit from the loan, they may levy a set-up fee and an annual management levy to cover administrative expenses. Such finance is only available to existing clients and is often used to ensure that those in financial difficulties can continue to honour existing financial commitments. It can also be provided as a stand-by facility to maintain third-party creditor confidence

riba   an addition to the principal of a loan, which

	is usually equated with interest. *Riba* is explicitly prohibited in the Quran (2: 275; 3: 130; 4: 161 and 30: 39) because it is viewed as exploitative
salam	an advance payment in full for a commodity for delivery at a future date. This contract was originally used for the financing of agricultural production with the advance payment being used by farmers to cover labour, seed, irrigation and other costs during planting and cultivation while benefiting from a fixed price on harvesting. As the payment is made in advance it is usually less than the expected spot price at the time of delivery. Today *salam* is used to finance the production of many commodities and is no longer confined to agricultural output. It is similar to a forward contract
Shari'ah	Islamic law based on the Divine guidance provided by the Quran and the *Sunnah*, the practices or 'way' of the Prophet during his life. This includes the Hadith, the narration of the Prophets rulings. For example, Imam Sahih Bukhari, one of the most respected early followers of Islam narrated what the Prophet ruled on loans, payment of loans, freezing of property and bankruptcy (Book 41)
sukuk	certificates of ownership or rights in tangible assets such as those being used as backing for an Islamic bond or floating-rate note
takaful	an Islamic alternative to a conventional insurance contract involving risk sharing by the participants rather than risk transfers. The collected funds are jointly owned by the

participants as in a mutual company but are used to cover individual losses

wakala an agency contract which provides for the appointment of a *wakeel* or agent to manage the financial assets of a person, family or business which continues to own the asset. The *wakeel* is paid a predetermined fixed fee rather than sharing in any profits generated by the assets as with a *mudarib*

zakat obligatory alms paid annually by Muslims according to the value of their wealth. The amount is usually calculated as one fortieth of the value of financial assets and excludes wealth in owner-occupied properties. Payment is viewed as one of the Five Pillars of Islam. Corporations, including Islamic banks, as well as individuals, have an obligation to pay *zakat*. The proceeds are used for charitable purposes to help the poor and needy with much of the expenditure devoted to health care and education for the underprivileged

INDEX